Karen Bro~

New England

Charming Inns & Itineraries

Written by

JACK BULLARD

Illustrations by Vanessa Kale
Cover Painting by Jann Pollard

Karen Brown's Guides, San Mateo, California

Karen Brown Titles

Austria: Charming Inns & Itineraries

California: Charming Inns & Itineraries

England: Charming Bed & Breakfasts

England, Wales & Scotland: Charming Hotels & Itineraries

France: Charming Bed & Breakfasts

France: Charming Inns & Itineraries

Germany: Charming Inns & Itineraries

Ireland: Charming Inns & Itineraries

Italy: Charming Bed & Breakfasts

Italy: Charming Inns & Itineraries

New England: Charming Inns & Itineraries

Portugal: Charming Inns & Itineraries

Spain: Charming Inns & Itineraries

Switzerland: Charming Inns & Itineraries

To each of you who have enriched my life in so many ways

through so many chapters

I thank you

The painting on the front cover is of Nantucket

Editors: Lorena Aburto, Clare Brown, June Brown, Karen Brown, Jack Bullard,
Cathy Knight, Iris Sandilands.

Illustrations: Vanessa Kale; Cover painting: Jann Pollard; Web designer: Lynn Upthagrove.

Maps: Susanne Lau Alloway—Greenleaf Design & Graphics

Copyright © 2001 by Karen Brown's Guides.

Distributed by Fodor's Travel Publications, Inc., 280 Park Avenue, New York, NY 10017, USA.

Distributed in the United Kingdom by Random House UK, 20 Vauxhall Bridge Road, London, SW1V 2SA, England, phone: 44 171 973 9000, fax: 44 171 840 8408.

Distributed in Australia by Random House Australia, 20 Alfred Street, Milsons Point, Sydney NSW 2061, Australia, phone: 61 2 9954 9966, fax: 61 2 9954 4562.

Distributed in New Zealand by Random House New Zealand, 18 Poland Road, Glenfield, Auckland, New Zealand, phone: 64 9 444 7197, fax: 64 9 444 7524.

Distributed in South Africa by Random House South Africa, Endulani, East Wing, 5A Jubilee Road, Parktown 2193, South Africa, phone: 27 11 484 3538, fax: 27 11 484 6180.

A catalog record for this book is available from the British Library.

Library of Congress Cataloging-in-Publication Data

Bullard, Jack, 1935-
    Karen Brown's New England : charming inns & itineraries / written by Jack Bullard ; illustrations by Vanessa Kale.
      p. cm. -- (Karen Brown's country inn series)
      ISBN 1-928901-12-3
    1. Bed and breakfast accommodations--New England--Guidebooks. 2. Hotels--New England--Guidebooks. 3. New England--Guidebooks. I. Brown, Karen, 1956- II. Title. III. Series.

    TX907.3. N35 B85 2000
    647.947401--dc21

                        00-037862

Contents

INTRODUCTION
    About This Guide   1
    About Inn Travel   2–9
    About Itineraries   10–14
    Overview Map of Driving Itineraries   15

ITINERARIES
    Boston: A Grand Beginning   16–22
    Cape Cod, Nantucket, Martha's Vineyard & Newport   23–30
    Sturbridge & the Connecticut Shore   31–36
    Route 7 & Much More   37–46
    The Byways of Coastal Maine   47–60
    Fall Foliage Routes with Overview Map   61–63
        Coastal & Central Maine   64–65
        Northern New Hampshire & Northern Vermont   66–68
        Southern Vermont   69
        Boston to Central Massachusetts   70
        Boston to Western Massachusetts   71
        Central & Western Connecticut   72–73
        Daytrip from Hartford   74

PLACES TO STAY
    Connecticut Inns   75–84
    Maine Inns   85–110
    Massachusetts Inns   111–144
    New Hampshire Inns   145–154
    Rhode Island Inns   155–160
    Vermont Inns   161–190

INDEX   191–199

Introduction

Because of its history, its special relationship with the sea, its back roads and scenic beauty, its changing seasons, and the great diversity between traveling the coast and the valleys and mountains, New England is a wonderful travel destination at all times of the year—though many consider that it is at its most glorious in the fall. New England is comprised of the six states in the northeast corner of the United States. The upper portion of New England encompasses Maine, New Hampshire, and Vermont, while Connecticut, Massachusetts, and Rhode Island make up the lower portion. The traveler to New England, more often than not, visits either the northern three states or the lower three since touring the entire region, with all its many and diverse attractions, requires a considerable investment of time.

About Inn Travel

We use the term "inn" to cover everything from a simple bed and breakfast to a sophisticated resort. A wide range of inns is included in this guide: some are great bargains, others very costly; some are in cities, others in remote locations; some are quite sophisticated, others extremely simple; some are decorated with opulent antiques, others with furniture from grandma's attic; some are large hotels, others have only a few rooms. The common denominator is that each place has some special quality that makes it appealing. The descriptions are intended to give you an honest appraisal of each property so that you can select accommodation based on personal preferences. The following pointers will help you appreciate and understand what to expect when traveling the "inn way."

BATHROOMS

Almost all the inns recommended in this book have an en-suite bathroom for each bedroom. Some inns will offer guestrooms that share a bath with other guestrooms, or rooms that have private baths down the hall. We make a note in the bottom details of the inn description if each guestroom does NOT have a private bathroom. We do not specify whether the bath is equipped with shower, tub-shower, tub, or Jacuzzi, so inquire what the term "with bathroom" means when making your reservation.

BREAKFAST

A welcome feature and trademark of many inns is their morning repast—many cookbooks have been authored and inspired by innkeepers. Breakfast is almost always included in the room rate, but we mention in the bottom details if it is NOT. Although innkeepers take great pride in their delectable morning offerings, know that breakfast can range from a gourmet "waddle away" feast (as proudly described by one innkeeper-chef) to muffins and coffee. Sometimes breakfast is limited to a Continental in the privacy of your room or a hot breakfast with others in the dining room, and sometimes both. Breakfast times vary as well—some innkeepers serve a hot breakfast at a specified time, while others replenish a buffet on a more leisurely schedule. Breakfasts are as individual as the inns themselves and are something to look forward to.

If you have any special dietary requirements, most innkeepers will gladly try to accommodate your needs. Not having a fully stocked refrigerator as a restaurant would have, innkeepers usually plan a breakfast menu that features one entree and have those ingredients on hand. Therefore, it is best to mention any special requests at the time of making your reservation both as a courtesy and from a practical point of view so that the innkeeper can have on hand items such as special low-fat dairy products, egg substitutes, sugar-free syrups, etc.

CANCELLATION POLICIES

Although policies vary, inns, by definition, have only a few rooms and when a reservation is made, the owner/innkeeper counts on receiving that revenue. Most inns usually require you to cancel at least a week in advance of the arrival date and some inns charge a small fee if the reservation is canceled in order to cover their administrative costs. If you cancel within a specified number of days prior to your planned arrival, you may be required to pay the first night if the room cannot be re-rented. Some inns have even more stringent policies, so be sure to enquire at the time you make your reservation.

CHECK-IN

Inns are usually very specific about check-in time—generally between 3 and 6 pm. Let the innkeeper know if you are going to arrive late and he will make special arrangements for you, such as leaving you a door key under a potted plant along with a note on how to find your room. Also, for those who might arrive early, note that some inns close their doors between check-out and check-in times. Inns are often frequently staffed only by the owners themselves and that window of time between check-out and check-in is often the only opportunity to shop for those wonderful breakfasts they prepare in addition to running their own personal errands.

CHILDREN

Many places in this guide cater only to adults and do not welcome children, or welcome children only over a certain age. They cannot legally refuse accommodation to children, but, as parents, we really want to know and want to stay where our children are genuinely welcome. Please enquire about the inn's policy when you make your reservation.

COMFORT

Comfort plays a deciding role in the selection of inns recommended. Firm mattresses, a quiet setting, good lighting, fresh towels, scrubbed bathrooms—we do our best to remember the basics when considering inns. The charming decor and innkeeper will soon be forgotten if you do not enjoy a good night's sleep and comfortable stay.

Be aware, however, that some inns in areas with hot summers, especially those in older buildings, do not always have the luxury of air conditioning. If air conditioning is of prime importance to you, ask if they have it when making a reservation.

CREDIT CARDS

Whether or not an establishment accepts credit cards is indicated at the bottom of each description—AX (American Express), MC (MasterCard), VS (Visa), all major, or none accepted. Even if an inn does not accept plastic payment, it will perhaps take your credit card as a guarantee of arrival.

CRITERIA FOR SELECTION

It is very important to us that an inn has charm—ideally an inn should be appealing, perhaps in an historic building, beautifully decorated, lovingly managed, and in a wonderful location. Few inns meet every criterion, but all our selections have something that makes them special and are situated in enjoyable surroundings—we have had to reject several lovely inns because of a poor location. Many are in historic buildings, but remember that the definition of "historic" may depend on the century in which the state came into being. Many inns are newly constructed and may be in buildings built to look old. Small inns are usually our favorites, but size alone did not dictate whether or not a hostelry was chosen. Most are small but sometimes the only place to stay in a "must-visit" area is a splendid, larger establishment of great character and charm. We have tried to include properties with a variety of size, decor, and ambiance to suit a variety of tastes and pocketbooks.

PROFESSIONALISM

The inns we have selected are run by professional innkeepers. There are many homes that rent out extra bedrooms to paying guests but this was not what we were looking for and they are not included in our guide. We have recommended only inns that have privacy for the guests and where you do not have to climb over family clutter to reach the bathroom.

RESERVATIONS

The best way to make a reservation is changing. We used to just pick up the phone and call but with the advent of the worldwide web, it is now possible to view many properties, including the bedrooms, "on line" and then make a reservation electronically. E-mail addresses are noted wherever available. Phoning is still a good way to discuss the various differences in available accommodation and the inn's policies. As a courtesy to the innkeepers, however, keep in mind that staff is often limited, and during certain periods of the day, such as the breakfast hour, they are busier than others—flipping pancakes, checking out guests, helping plan activities. Also, inns are often homes, and you might be waking up the innkeeper if you call late evenings or early mornings. Another convenient and efficient way to request a reservation is by fax: if the inn has a fax, we have noted the number in the information line next to the telephone number. As a final note: When planning your trip, be aware that the majority of inns in this guide require a two-night stay on weekends and over holidays.

RESPONSIBILITY

Our goal is to outline itineraries in regions that we consider of prime interest to our readers and to recommend inns that we think are outstanding. All of the inns featured have been selected solely on their merits. Our judgments are made on the charm of the inn, its setting, cleanliness, and, above all, the warmth of welcome. Each property has its own appeal, and we try to present you with a very honest appraisal. However, no matter how careful we are, sometimes we misjudge an inn's merits, or the ownership changes, or unfortunately sometimes inns just do not maintain their standards. If you find an inn is not as we have indicated, please let us know, and accept our sincere apologies.

Introduction–About Inn Travel

RESTAURANTS

A bonus to staying in a New England inn is that of dining in its restaurant. Your meal will be a great one and will feature regional fare ranging from seafood like lobster, clams, and bluefish to the wild game of pheasant and quail. The heritage of New England is turkey and Thanksgiving dinners generally include the presentation of this bird with a variety of family stuffing recipes, from oyster to corn bread to traditional herb bread with seasonings. At the end of a day of touring you'll find that the fireplace in the inn's tavern and another in the dining room will lure you to both warmth and good dining.

ROOM RATES

It seems that many inns play musical rates, with high-season, low-season, midweek, weekend, and holiday rates. We have quoted the 2001 high-season, general range of rates from the lowest-priced bedroom for two people (singles usually receive a very small discount) to the most expensive suite, including breakfast. The rates given are those quoted to us by the inn. Please use these figures as a guideline and be certain to ask at the time of booking what the rates are and what they include. We have not given prices for "special" rooms such as those that can accommodate three people traveling together. Discuss with the innkeeper rooms and rates available before making your selection. Of course, several inns are exceptions to our guidelines and whenever this is the case we mention the special situation (such as breakfast not being included in the rate). Please be aware that local tourist taxes are not included in the rates quoted and can be very high—frequently around 10%.

SMOKING

Most inns have extremely strict non-smoking policies. A few inns permit smoking in restricted public areas or outside, but in general it is best to assume that smoking is not appropriate. If smoking is of great concern, be sure to ask the hotel specifically as to their policy about smoking in the garden, on the deck, or in a specially designated public area.

SOCIALIZING

Inns usually offer a conviviality rarely found in a "standard" hotel. The gamut runs all the way from playing "cozy family" around the kitchen table to sharing a sophisticated, elegant cocktail hour in the parlor. Breakfast may be a formal meal served at a set hour when the guests gather around the dining-room table, or it may be served buffet-style over several hours where guests have the option of either sitting down to eat alone or joining other guests at a larger table. Then again, some inns will bring a breakfast tray to

Introduction–About Inn Travel

your room, or perhaps breakfast in the room is the only option. After check-in, many inns offer afternoon refreshment, such as tea and cakes or wine and hors d'oeuvres, which may be seen as another social opportunity. Some inns set out the refreshments buffet-style where guests are invited to meander in and out mixing or not mixing with other guests as they choose and then others orchestrate a more structured gathering, often a social hour, with the innkeeper presiding. Choose the inn that seems to offer the degree of togetherness or privacy that you desire.

WEBSITE

We are constantly changing and updating the Karen Brown website with the aim of providing an enhanced extension of our guides and supplying you with even more information on the properties and destinations that we recommend. Many inns that we work very closely with, and who opt to participate, are featured on our website—their web addresses are detailed on the description pages. We will continue to add photos for as many properties as possible and you will be able to link directly to the inns' individual websites, if available, for their personal photos and more information. On our site we share comments, feedback, and discoveries from you, our readers, and keep you informed of our latest finds, current updates, and special offers. We want our website to serve as a valuable and added dimension to our guides. Be sure to visit us at *www.karenbrown.com*.

WHEELCHAIR ACCESSIBILITY

If an inn has *at least* one guestroom that is accessible by wheelchair, it is noted as having a handicap room in the details listed at the end of the description. Because the term is vague, depending on your own needs, be sure to question the hotel, inn or B&B in more detail as to the type and specifics of accessibility they offer.

About Itineraries

Though the same thread of culture described by many as "Yankee" is woven throughout all six states, there are distinctive differences between the states themselves, and within each state there are areas that are markedly different in terrain, weather patterns, and tourist attractions. These differences make for delightful trips and this book guides you on journeys that show off this diversity and give you the opportunity to choose the experiences you most want to have.

Five detailed driving itineraries describe routes through the various regions of New England so that you can choose a journey through an area that appeals both to your time and travel parameters and one that includes the places you have your heart set on visiting. In addition, we include routes for seven fall foliage tours. Each itinerary is preceded by a map that shows the routing and all the towns in which we have a recommended inn or sightseeing. Two overview maps (one of the regional itineraries and one of the fall foliage tours) help you tailor these itineraries to meet your own specific needs by leaving out some sightseeing if time is limited, or linking several itineraries together if you wish to enjoy a longer vacation.

Though several itineraries use Boston as their point of origination and this is a logical starting point for travel to Cape Cod and the Berkshires, they may be accessed at any point en route and from any of the various points at which you may arrive in the northeast. Your entry into New England will probably depend on your destination—Manchester, New Hampshire for ease of access into Maine, New Hampshire, and Vermont; Providence, Rhode Island for visiting Cape Cod, the islands of Nantucket and Martha's Vineyard, and the small but activity-rich areas of Rhode Island; Hartford, Connecticut for trips to the western portions of Connecticut and Massachusetts and north into Vermont and New Hampshire; and Albany, New York for alternative access to the western parts of New England. Although New York City is located at least an hour's drive (more if you travel during congested commuter hours) from Connecticut and the start of the itinerary traveling up the western side of New England, its airports may provide the best airfares and schedules for the international as well as the more distant U.S. traveler.

ANTIQUING

If you have a passion for antiquing, you might already know that New England is full of treasures to satisfy almost any desire to start or add to a collection. Most of the antique shops in New England are small and privately owned, but in the last several years "collectives" have become very popular. These are group shops representing a few antique dealers or maybe as many as a hundred—obviously, in the larger shops there is a greater chance of finding the elusive object you're searching for. Antiques are generally divided into objects of significant value and collectibles, the latter having less dollar value but not necessarily less interest value to the buyer. Fortunately, in New England there is a wealth of both antiques and collectibles and the real challenge is finding the shops in which those treasures you have always wanted will be waiting for you. To aid you in this, the best reference book is Sloan's *Green Guide to Antiquing in New England* (ISBN 0-7627-0162-5), a compendium of 2,500 shops. Remember that any dealer generally has in stock something that he has acquired that is not within his general line of expertise—in that case you have an opportunity to purchase a bargain, since no antique dealer can be familiar with the value of all objects in all categories.

CAR RENTAL

Our itineraries are designed for travel by car. If you are staying in any of the major cities at the beginning of your trip, it is not necessary to pick up a rental car until you leave the city or just before any day trips you can only make by car, since public transportation systems are so convenient and all of the cities are great for walking. Ask your hotel if there is a car rental office nearby—if so, you might find out if that particular company can give you rates as good as any other. If you are really lucky, as with at least one of the rental companies, you might even have your car delivered to your hotel. There is no question that the less time you have to spend getting to your car and then turning it in at the end of your trip, the happier you will be. Inquire when you make your car reservation about all the add-on charges, and don't be surprised at how much they increase the total rental cost. Do check to see if your home or car insurance or your credit card will provide you with coverage in the event of an accident.

DRIVING TIMES

New England is not particularly large—in the central portions six hours of driving will generally take you from east to west or from south to north unless you stretch out New England and try to go from southern Connecticut to the tip of Maine (more like a ten-hour trip). We have indicated in our itineraries a daily pace that we believe will make for a pleasant and comfortable trip, allowing you time to enjoy not only the scenery but also the historic sights along the way. Allow more time if you want to do a lot of shopping or if you have a special interest in any particular area.

MAPS

Each itinerary has a map outlining the suggested routing and marking sightseeing and overnight stops. Alternative places to stay are also marked. The maps are an artist's rendering and do not show every road and highway—you need to supplement them with more comprehensive commercial maps.

PACING

At the beginning of each itinerary we suggest our recommended pacing to help you decide the amount of time to allocate to each one. The suggested time frame reflects how much there is to see and do. Use our recommendation as a guideline only, and choreograph your own itinerary based on how much leisure time you have and whether your preference is to move on to a new destination each day or to settle in and use a particular inn as your base.

WEATHER

There's a saying in New England that if you don't like the weather, just wait a few minutes. While the weather may be changeable, there are certainly some guidelines that will be helpful to the traveler. In the winter months of December through March, you can expect everything from snow and ice to sleet and freezing rain. Temperatures often get down to zero and below, and there may be days and even weeks when there is little snow and just brisk cold weather. Traditionally, in the latter half of January there is even a period of warm weather, deceiving everyone into believing that winter is over. The spring months of April, May, and June are wonderful, with all of New England sprouting forth with bulbs of every description and flowering shrubs and trees. The newness of everything with the freshness of spring green is hard not to love. Occasionally, however, in the spring, there is a taste of winter weather that will remind you that the decision to bring a coat on your trip was indeed a very good one. Summer is a lazy time of year and generally has lovely weather, but there will be rain showers. Summer can also get hot and humid—on those days you'll welcome the pair of shorts and short-sleeved shirt that you brought and you'll be grateful that your rental car and your hotel are air-conditioned. Many a traveler will say that New England is best in the fall when the days are long and warm, the evenings are cool, and the foliage begins to turn.

Introduction–About Itineraries

Overview Map of Driving Itineraries

Bar Harbor

Shelburne

Byways of Coastal Maine

Manchester
Center

*Route 7 &
Much More*

Sturbridge

Boston

*Sturbridge & the
Connecticut Shore*

Newport

Chatham

Old Lyme

Mystic

*Cape Cod, Nantucket,
Martha's Vineyard & Newport*

Norwalk

15

Boston: A Grand Beginning

Boston, the economic and intellectual center of New England and, historically, America's cradle of liberty, is the stage on which much of the drama of the earliest years of our country took place. It is here that the Colonies, which evolved into the present United States, were first established. The capitol city of Massachusetts, **Boston** was first settled in the 17th century but it was the 18th century that saw the growing rift between the English Parliament and the colonists in what was referred to as the Bay Colony. Many of the historic sites and buildings in Boston and the towns surrounding it are associated with this period of separation from the Crown.

Beaconhill, Acorn Street

Recommended Pacing: Plan to spend at least three nights and four full days in Boston, and you will be able to pick and choose among the many things to do and come up with a program tailored to your interests. Touring Boston is not only desirable but really a necessary element to fully experience New England. In fact, if you want to see in depth all that's here in the way of historical, cultural, and educational importance, you may never leave Boston at all!

Getting Around: Boston has a good public transportation system, so the best way to explore the city is by subway. Visit Park Street station, one of the main downtown stations, to obtain a map of the color-coded subway lines and information on Boston Passports, which provide unlimited subway travel for 1, 3, 5, and 7 days. If you are planning on taking day trips to Lexington or Marblehead, you can do so from North Station (on the subway system). For further information, contact *www.boston.com/travel*. Do not pick up a rental car until you leave the city.

In Boston you should not miss walking along the **Freedom Trail** in the heart of the city, marked by a red brick path in the pavement (this takes at least two hours). The trail leads to the sites where many of the history-making events that created the new country took place—be sure to include the **Old South Meeting House**, the **Old State House**, **Faneuil Hall**, and **Quincy Market**. A detour onto **Beacon Hill**, an area where early merchants built homes and where the **Capitol Building** is located, is well worth the time. If you would like to do some shopping as a break from all the history, just walk across the Boston Common and proceed with credit card in hand down **Newbury Street** where you find the city's finest boutiques, art galleries, and some of the best restaurants.

Old State House

Charles Bullfinch, one of the principal architects of many of Boston's historic buildings, completed the **State House**, with its golden dome, in 1786. Nearby, another example of his talent, the **Harrison Gray Otis House**, today serves as the headquarters of **SPNEA** (Society for the Preservation of New England Antiquities). Throughout New England there are 37 houses and gardens owned by SPNEA, displaying the furnishings and decorative arts of the region's past. Telephone (617) 227-3956 or visit their website at *www.spnea.com* for information on these historic properties.

The State House

Boston: A Grand Beginning

Back Bay, with its commercial and shopping areas, begins at the **Boston Common**, a 50-acre park in the center of the city. The adjacent **Boston Garden**, with its guide-pedaled swan boats, is a treat for the children who have read and loved *Make Way for Ducklings*. Noteworthy in Back Bay are **Copley Square**, **Trinity Church**, and the **John Hancock Tower** from which views can be had in all directions. **Commonwealth Avenue** retains much of the grandeur of a residential street with its center mall lined with elm trees.

In the colorful part of Boston known as the **North End** there are many Italian bakeries, restaurants, and street markets. The **Paul Revere House**, downtown Boston's only 17th-century house (now a museum), was the starting point for his famous ride to Lexington and Concord to warn the patriots of the coming of the British.

Boston's **financial district** is centered around one of its major transportation hubs, South Station. Within a few blocks' walk are the Aquarium, Chinatown, the theatre district, and many shopping opportunities in the larger department stores.

Boston, home since the early years to some of our nation's most prominent educational, medical, and research institutions, is equally famous for its cultural activities. Here you find important international museums including the **Museum of Fine Arts** and the **Isabella Stewart Gardner Museum**. While each is very different from the other, they both have world-renowned art comparable to the best museums anywhere. In the Museum of Fine Arts, our favorite galleries would include those devoted to American and European art, but major collections of Asiatic, Egyptian, Nubian, and Near-Eastern artworks, as well as sculpture and photography, are there to enjoy. At the neighboring Isabella Stewart Gardner Museum, the art objects collected by Mrs. Gardner are displayed exactly as they were in her lifetime, making a tour of this museum a very intimate experience. At the heart of the museum you find a renowned courtyard with plantings changed throughout the seasons and concerts are held regularly in the Tapestry Room. Just south of the city, reachable via public transportation, is the **Museum at the John Fitzgerald Kennedy Library**, which houses the archives of the former president.

Back Bay skyline and the Charles River

For children there are two museums of particular note. The **Boston Museum of Science**, located in a building on the Charles River, offers an educational array of exhibits that invite active participation in the world of science and technology. This museum is fascinating and I urge you to make time for it in your program. The **Children's Museum** at Museum Wharf is a wonderful, interactive, educational museum that will delight adults as well as children and also has an area for toddlers and preschoolers.

The **Boston Symphony Orchestra**, one of the world's most famous, performs throughout the fall, winter and spring seasons in Symphony Hall and during the summer at Tanglewood in the Berkshires. The **Boston Pops**, with its programs of lighter music, performs in summer at Symphony Hall and in free concerts on the Charles River

Esplanade. There's nothing like a summer night under the stars listening to music with a picnic supper—I suggest that you bring a blanket and enjoy this very special treat. Boston has a **theatre district** just south of Boston Common and not far from the financial district—most of the theatres are on Tremont and Boylston Streets. Here you can find many pre-Broadway and current Broadway shows, as well as a ballet company, which performs seasonally.

Across the river, neighboring **Cambridge** is home to **Harvard University, Radcliffe College**, and the **Massachusetts Institute of Technology**. Around these academic communities has developed a maze of commercial and residential neighborhoods, artists' studios, and theatres. On the Harvard campus, sites worth visiting include **Harvard Yard** with its student residential buildings, **Memorial Church, Harvard Museums of Cultural and Natural History,** and the **Botanical Museum,** which houses the world-renowned collection of Blashka glass flowers. These pieces were created between 1877 and 1936, and represent more than 780 species of flowering plants—an absolute must for garden enthusiasts. To this day no one has been able to recreate the processes used in producing these magnificent examples of floral beauty.

For adults and children alike, the **New England Aquarium** is a special place to visit. Its center exhibit is a four-story 187,000-gallon ocean tank recreating a Caribbean reef and there are also exhibits encouraging children to handle crabs, sea urchins, and starfish.

The *USS Constitution*, the oldest commissioned warship afloat, which participated in a number of sea battles in disputes between the American colonies and the British, is berthed in Charlestown and reached using public transportation unless you are up for a very long walk.

There are many other varied attractions for the visitor to Boston. More information can be obtained from the **Greater Boston Convention and Visitors Bureau** located at 2 Copley Place, Suite 105 (tel: 1-888-SEE BOSTON, web page: *www.bostonusa.com*) and at the intersection of Tremont and West Streets.

We recommend two hotels in Boston—**The Charles Street Inn** and **The Lenox**. Full descriptions and details are given in the *Massachusetts Places to Stay* section of this book.

Sand dunes on the Massachusetts shore

Boston: A Grand Beginning

Cape Cod, Nantucket,
Martha's Vineyard & Newport

- ● Places to Stay
- ○ Orientation/Sightseeing
- ▬ Itinerary Route

Boston
Quincy
Cohasset
3A
3
95
Duxbury
Plymouth
Provincetown
Cape Cod Nat'l. Seashore
6
Sandwich
Providence
Wareham
25
6A
Barnstable
Brewster
Eastham
Dennis
Orleans
95
6
Hyannis
Chatham
95
195
Yarmouth Port
138
South Yarmouth
95
Woods Hole
28
Falmouth
138
114
Vineyard
Haven
Newport
Oak Bluffs
Gay Head
Edgartown
Martha's Vineyard

Nantucket Island

Nantucket
Wauwinet

23

Cape Cod, Nantucket,
Martha's Vineyard & Newport

Travel south from Boston to the coastal villages and fishing harbors of Cape Cod, out to the enticing islands of Nantucket and Martha's Vineyard, on to the gracious mansions of Newport, and back to Boston. Along the way you have ample opportunities for antiquing and you'll come to love the weathered architecture that gave its name to the "Cape" style of building. The north shore of the Cape along Route 6A is my favorite—it's much quieter, less populated, and much less commercial than the towns along Route 28 to the south and there is a real sense of community here. Flower gardens thrive on Cape Cod in the warm months, especially the roses, which seem almost to engulf the houses in early June.

Nantucket

Recommended Pacing: This itinerary can be comfortably followed in its entirety in five or six nights though you can of course adapt it to fit your individual interests. On day one head south along the coastal route, visit Hingham, Duxbury, and Plymouth, cross the Sagamore Bridge, and stay overnight in Sandwich. On day two drive along the north side of Cape Cod to the Cape Cod National Seashore and the artist community of Provincetown, spending the night in Orleans, Eastham or Chatham. Day three takes you south along the coast to Hyannis, from where you take the ferry or fly to the islands of Nantucket or Martha's Vineyard. A day, minimum, on each of these islands provides time to see the villages and to absorb the culture of the seafarers who arrived as early as the 18th century. On day five a flight or boat trip back to Hyannis and a drive to Newport, Rhode Island provide an opportunity to see the grand summer cottages of the "rich and famous" residents who built in the first quarter of the 19th century. Spend the night in Newport and then a second night if your interest in touring the mansions of Newport has absorbed an entire day. From Newport head north back to Boston, stopping off en route to explore Providence, the capitol of Rhode Island.

The Cape Cod Canal is only an hour's drive from Boston if you take the Southeast Expressway out of Boston and pick up Route 3 to the Cape. The bridge onto Cape Cod can also can be reached via the winding Route 3A, a slower road, which takes you through the coastal communities whose history and charm will make their way into your heart. (Note that the towns located along the 3A and Cape Cod are best and most easily visited outside commuter hours.) From Boston follow signs onto the Southeast Expressway (I-93) to Quincy and then take either the faster Route 3 or the more leisurely Route 3A to the Sagamore Bridge and the beginning of the Cape.

On Route 3A the towns of **Quincy, Cohasset, Duxbury,** and **Plymouth** are quaint: their main streets have been traveled for the last two centuries by horse, carriage, and now suburban utility vehicle. It is worthwhile to stop in Plymouth at the historical sites of **Plymouth Rock,** where the Pilgrims first landed, and the replica of **Mayflower II,** the ship that brought the Pilgrims to Plymouth in 1620. There are two museums, the **Mayflower Society Museum** and the **Pilgrim Hall Museum.**

The **Sagamore Bridge** spans the **Cape Cod Canal**, which is used by shipping and pleasure craft to avoid circumnavigating the entire Cape on journeys between Boston and the coasts of Rhode Island, Connecticut, and states to the south. This is your entrance onto **Cape Cod** with its scenic character and unique charm. Almost immediately after crossing the bridge, exit Route 6 (the continuation of Route 3) onto Route 130 then 6A to the town of **Sandwich**, an excellent place to stop for the night (be sure to make advance reservations in season.) The town is a charming one for wandering the streets and has two outstanding museums. The **Sandwich Glass Museum** (closed in January) displays the glass produced in Sandwich between 1825 and 1888—lamps, candlesticks, tiebacks, doorknobs, vases, etc in various colors, which have become collectors' treasures. The **Heritage Plantation Museum**, founded with the generous contributions of the Lily family, has collections of early-American historical artifacts and folk art. There are extensive collections of firearms, cars, and folk art and an old-fashioned carousel. On the museum's grounds is an extensive rhododendron garden, which blooms each year from mid-May to mid-June—a "must" if you have an interest in gardening.

Leaving Sandwich, get onto Route 6A, the northern route along the upper coast of Cape Cod. It's a delightful road to follow as it winds its way through the lovely, historical towns of **Barnstable**, **Yarmouth Port**, **Dennis**, and **Brewster**. These old seafaring communities with their lovely main streets, beautiful homes, and colorful harbors make for a wonderful day of browsing, antiquing, and just plain absorbing the atmosphere of the Cape. Continuing north through the towns of **Orleans** and **Eastham**, you come to the **Cape Cod National Seashore** where you can take a fabulous dunes tour from April through October—a perfect way to see the ever-changing face of the sand dunes of this portion of the Cape. Farther on, at the tip of the Cape, is the artist community of **Provincetown. Chatham**, protected by the sandy offshore barrier of Nauset Beach, remains an active fishing port.

Head south and travel along the south shore of Cape Cod on Route 28, which brings you into the more commercial area of the Cape—more traffic, more shops, and more restaurants but also many inns and places to visit. **Hyannis** is the major shopping center for Cape Cod's residents and also the **summer home** of former president **John F. Kennedy** where there is a small museum of photographs of the Kennedy family on summer vacations.

Nauset Light, Eastham

Before you return to the mainland take the time to visit the enchanting islands of Nantucket and Martha's Vineyard. Leave your car in the parking lot at any one of the various departure points (Hyannis, Woods Hole, Falmouth, or New Bedford) from which airplane or ferry services, but not necessarily both, are available. Some ferries are catamarans and make very fast trips. The frequency of both air and ferry service depends on the season and the weather (on the day I was to go to Nantucket, fog prevented me from flying and I ended up taking the one-hour ferry from Hyannis). You can fly to Nantucket or Martha's Vineyard from Hyannis (the best and most frequent service), Providence, and Boston with Cape Air (800-352-0714), Island Airline (800-249-7779), and US Airways (800-428-4322). Ferries to Nantucket run from Hyannis (alternative departure points include Harwich Port and Martha's Vineyard). Hy-Line (508-778-2600) has a one-hour high-speed catamaran and the Steamship Authority runs a high-speed catamaran and other boats that take somewhat longer (508-495-FAST). Ferries to Martha's Vineyard leave from Falmouth, Hyannis, Woods Hole, New Bedford, and Nantucket. I suggest that you ask the staff at the inn at which you are planning to stay for their recommendation of the best and fastest routes.

The two offshore islands of Nantucket and Martha's Vineyard were major whaling industry seaports from 1740 to 1830. Wealthy tradesmen associated with this very profitable venture built many of the magnificent homes along the streets of the seafaring ports of both islands.

Nantucket is perfect for exploring on foot or by bicycle (bicycles may easily be rented from one of the many shops near the ferry landing.) The **Nantucket Historical Association** sells combination tickets to the historic houses and museums it manages, which include the **Whaling Museum,** the **Old Mill** (a 1746 windmill still being used to grind corn), **Old Gaol** (the original jail with its four cells), and the **Oldest House** on the island. Tickets are available at any of these locations. Along the town of Nantucket's cobblestoned, elm-shaded Main Street are many shops, art galleries, and very good restaurants, the latter specializing in the locally caught seafood. Of particular note are the **Three Bricks**, three stately mansions built by a wealthy merchant for his three sons. Nantucket is one of my all-time favorite places—I have been there in the summer; I have enjoyed vacation in a rented cottage in October; and I have spent a New Year's weekend there. Each occasion was very special. Nantucket is simply one of those destinations whose ambiance and charm vary with the mood of the season—it is improved only by your having more time to spend there.

When it comes time to leave Nantucket, go on to Martha's Vineyard by boat or by plane or return to the mainland.

Martha's Vineyard has a greater number of villages to visit so unless you are going to restrict your visit to the village where the ferry docks, you will either have to rent a car (my suggestion if you are planning to spend more than just a brief visit) or take taxis to reach the various parts of the island. Of course, you can also rent a bicycle but remember that the villages, which appear to be so close together on the map, are really several to many miles apart. If you fly to Martha's Vineyard, you will need to rent a car since the airport is some distance from the island's points of interest.

The ferry (from Wood's Hole, Hyannis, Falmouth, or Nantucket) will bring you into one of the three principal villages on Martha's Vineyard. Vineyard Haven, Oak Bluffs, and Edgartown are distinctly different from one another, although they are all fishing villages. **Vineyard Haven**, the principal entry point to the Vineyard and a source of rental cars or bicycles for touring the island, has a group of shops and restaurants but quite quickly changes into a rural landscape stretching along the coast with homes built within the last century. There is particular charm in the settlement of **Oak Bluffs**, a meeting place for Methodists in the late 19th and early 20th centuries. Around the meeting ground and the tabernacle that was built for these religious gatherings, a colony of small wooden cottages decorated with gingerbread (Victorian lace-like) trim were built and painted in wonderfully vivid colors. **Edgartown** was the seaport from which the whalers left to hunt the elusive whale, and the island's mansions were built in this area. Be sure to visit **Gay Head** with its clay cliffs that have stood high above the sea for the last 100 million years—their colors and majesty are memorable.

Returning either by boat or by plane to the mainland, drive west on Route 28 through Falmouth, picking up Route 25, which in turn connects to I-195. Look for the exit to Route 136 south and then Route 114 into **Newport**, Rhode Island. The homes built there in the 19th century for the wealthy to escape the oppressive summer heat of the south became the center of a social life never seen before or since. Today many of these homes are open to the public and tours give you a glimpse of the opulence of a bygone era. You can tour many of these homes and if you plan on visiting several, purchase a ticket that will allow you to visit two or eight of them. Among the "must-visit" mansions are The Breakers, home of Cornelius Vanderbilt, The Marble House, built for William Vanderbilt, The Elms, and Rosecliff, used for the filming of *The Great Gatsby*. For details and tickets call (401) 847-1000.

Take a bracing walk along the oceanfront, which enhances the image of those halcyon days. This is a very special experience; and you should plan to take an hour or several hours, perhaps as I did with a bottle of wine, some cheese, and a loaf of good bread, to enjoy this oceanfront path. With the ocean on one side and the fabulous homes on the other, this is a memorable experience. Today many festivals take place in Newport, including a music festival during the summer months.

Leaving Newport, head back north on Routes 114 and 136 to I-195 into **Providence**. This is the capitol city of Rhode Island with its capitol building standing high on a hill as you travel north. Here the educational institutions of **Brown University** and the **Rhode Island School of Design** are located in a tree-shaded residential neighborhood where there are many small cafés, bookstores, and little shops. At the Rhode Island School of Design there is a museum with collections ranging from medieval to contemporary and in the nearby **John Brown House** you can take a guided tour of this 18th-century brick museum with its fabulous collection of furniture belonging to the family.

Leaving Providence, drive north on I-95 to Route 128, the circumferential route around the city of Boston and follow the signs to Boston. This is about an hour's drive unless you hit rush hour.

If you plan to connect with another of the itineraries in the southern part of New England, drive south and west from the Providence area on I-95 along the coast of Connecticut into the area of the Connecticut River Valley.

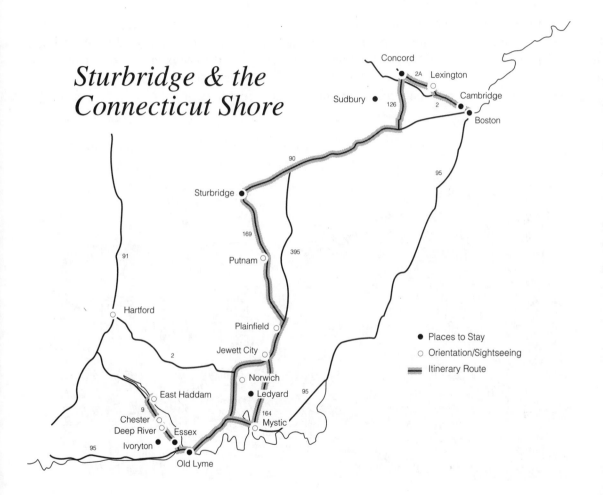

Sturbridge & the Connecticut Shore

Concord

2A Lexington

Sudbury

126

2

Cambridge

Boston

90

95

Sturbridge

169

395

Putnam

91

Hartford

Plainfield

2

Jewett City

Norwich

East Haddam

● Places to Stay

○ Orientation/Sightseeing

▬▬ Itinerary Route

Ledyard

95

9

Chester

164

Deep River

Essex

Mystic

95

Ivoryton

Old Lyme

Sturbridge & the Connecticut Shore

This itinerary takes the traveler from Boston to Lexington and Concord, sites of historical events which led to the founding of the Colonies, and from there westward to Sturbridge Village and south to the Connecticut shoreline, with a visit to Mystic Seaport. This is an especially good route for those with children since the historical sites have guides who theatrically depict the events that took place in days now long gone.

Mystic

Recommended Pacing: The Lexington and Concord portion of this itinerary is an easy day trip from Boston since this area is only about an hour's drive from the city. Alternatively, you can overnight here or go on to Sturbridge, a little less than an hour away, and sleep there. Plan on spending one full day in Sturbridge before heading for the Connecticut shore, about an hour and a half beyond Sturbridge.

Lexington and Concord are today residential suburbs of Boston, but their place in history has linked them together for over 200 years. It was here in April 1775 that the Colonial troops fought with the British in skirmishes that eventually led to the **American Revolution**. That story comes alive in the preservation of the sites and monuments, and in the annual April 19th re-creation of those most important events. In areas now designated as national parks, guides relate the events that led to the revolution to give the visitor, young and old, a graphic understanding of what took place during that momentous time. Perhaps the most famous story is that of **Paul Revere's** horseback ride from Boston to Lexington and Concord to warn of the impending attack by the British, which enabled the colonists to meet the challenge and drive them back.

To reach Lexington, leave Boston on Storrow Drive and then follow signs to Route 2, which takes you from Boston west through Cambridge and Arlington. Exit Route 2 in Arlington on Route 60 to Route 2A, which will take you into the center of **Lexington**. Lexington's village green, with its several monuments to the April 19 rout of the British who fled back to Boston, is surrounded by lovely homes and there are a few shops and restaurants where you can refresh yourself after walking around the historic area.

Leaving Lexington, continue along Route 2A to **Concord** and visit the area where the battle at the **Old North Bridge** between the British and the Minutemen took place. The **Minutemen**, so called because of their willingness to pick up arms on a minute's notice to defend against injustices inflicted by the British government, drove the British soldiers back through Lexington and on to Boston. At the **Old North Bridge Visitor Center** there is a replica of the "bridge that arched the flood" and a national park ranger tells the story.

The **Minuteman National Historic Park** between the towns of Lexington, Lincoln, and Concord has a Minuteman Visitor Center showing a movie that re-creates that time.

The Old North Bridge

The **Concord Museum** in the town center houses 19 galleries with furnishings of the revolutionary period and the century that followed. What is particularly interesting in this museum is that each room represents a different period. As you tour these various rooms, guides explain the evolving style of decoration and life as it was lived at that time. Other interesting stops include **Orchard House**, home of Louisa May Alcott, author of *Little Women*, the home of the poet **Ralph Waldo Emerson**, and **Walden Pond** where Henry David Thoreau lived and wrote. **Sleepy Hollow Cemetery**, the ancient burial ground for many of these famous citizens, is a suitable finale to the Concord tour.

From Concord Route 126 leads south to the Massachusetts Turnpike (I-90), which is the fastest way to reach **Sturbridge**, less than an hour away. You should allow a full day to explore **Old Sturbridge Village**, a re-creation of life as lived in the first half of the 19th century. There are more than 40 staffed exhibits, homes, craft shops, mills, and farm buildings on more than 200 acres of fields and farmland. Among my favorite buildings is the clock gallery where many different types of timepieces are on display. In addition to the one-room schoolhouse, the mills, and the demonstrations of shoemaking and cooking over a wood fire, there are seasonal exhibits of sheep shearing, apple pressing, and maple sugaring. For children there is a special educational program providing hands-on activities. Be sure to wear comfortable walking shoes.

From Sturbridge the scenic Route 169 leads south toward the Connecticut shore. However, if time is of the essence, I would recommend Route 20 from Sturbridge northeast to Auburn, picking up I-395 south to Jewett City and then Route 164 into **Mystic Village Seaport** a stop that appeals to both parents and children alike. Ever since the 17th century Mystic has been the center of shipbuilding and of maritime commerce. It is now a museum village depicting life as it was in this earlier time. At the visitor center a movie is shown that introduces you to the town—an excellent way to begin your visit. Many clipper ships were built in this port in the middle of the 19th century and here you find several examples of the vessels of that era. Of the three fully rigged sailing craft moored at the docks, particularly interesting—and open for tours—is the ***Charles W. Morgan***, the last of the 19th-century whaling ships surviving today. Don't miss the shops of the craftsmen who made the materials used in the construction and the sailing of these vessels. There is a **Children's Museum** where you can enjoy the activities and games played on board ship. In the **Stillman Building** visitors can watch a ten-minute film describing the adventure of whale hunting on the open sea.

If you have time, a drive through the **Connecticut River Valley** is most relaxing. To reach the towns along the Connecticut River take I-95 south to Route 9 north and exit immediately for Essex. The valley has along its banks a number of lovely Colonial seafaring towns where white clapboard homes, churches, and town greens are very much in evidence. There are old shops and pubs, and a number of art galleries reflecting the love that so many artists have for this area. Be sure to visit **Essex** and drive the broad tree-lined main streets of **Lyme** and **Old Lyme**. In season there is a steam train running from Essex to **Chester**, about an hour's trip, enabling you to enjoy the Connecticut River Valley at its best. A riverboat trip from **Deep River** to **East Haddam** can be either a separate trip or combined with the train excursion. In the town of East Haddam, during the months of April through December, the **Goodspeed Opera House** is the home of musicals being tried out for the legitimate theatre and revivals of some of America's most beloved plays.

You have several options at the end of this itinerary: return to Boston going northeast on I-95 along the Connecticut and Rhode Island coasts through Providence (about two and a half hours); go north to I-91 to visit northern New England; or travel west on I-95 along the coast of lower Connecticut to Norwalk where you can join the itinerary *Route 7 & Much More* through the western part of Connecticut, Massachusetts, and Vermont. If you are leaving New England, continue southwest along the I-95 to the airports of La Guardia and Kennedy.

**Route 7 &
Much More**

- ● Places to Stay
- ○ Orientation/Sightseeing
- ▨ Itinerary Route

Craftsbury Common
Burlington
Shelburne
Montpelier
St Johnsbury
Lower Waterford
89
14
2
91
Waitsfield
Warren
Middlebury
7
Chelsea
100
Goshen
Brandon
Chittenden
Mendon
Rutland
Barnard
Woodstock
89
12
Bridgewater Corners
Weston
Ludlow
Perkinsville
Londonderry
Dorset
Andover
Manchester Cntr.
Grafton
103
191
Manchester
35
West Townshend
Jamaica
Townshend
Arlington
100
Newfane
Bennington
9
30
Williamstown
West Dover
Brattleboro
Pittsfield
7
Lenox
Stockbridge
Springfield
Great Barrington
South Egremont
Sheffield
Ashley Falls
91
Salisbury
Norfolk
Cornwall Bridge
63
341
Litchfield
7
New Preston
Hartford
New Milford
202
84
15
91
New Haven
Ridgefield
7
New Canaan
15
95
Westport
Norwalk

Green Mountain Nat'l. Forest

Route 7 & Much More

A trip to New England should include a drive along the western edge of the region through the states of Connecticut, Massachusetts, and Vermont. Fortunately, Route 7 follows the contours of this western edge almost exactly and is the backbone of this itinerary. The "much more" portion comes when you cross the Green Mountains to visit the towns of Newfane, Townshend, and West Townshend. If you're interested in antiques, there is no drive with more "opportunities" waiting than this one. If what appeals to you is the charm of countryside, field, and farm, the rural character of this route will delight you. Pretty little towns appearing around bends in the road after miles of countryside present farmhouses, stately mansions, and summer cottages—each with its own brand of charm. Plan on being in one of these towns to share the experience of Memorial Day or the Fourth of July when the schoolchildren parade, the girl and boy scouts march, the high-school band plays, the hardware store mans a float, and the fire engine screams its presence.

Route 7 & Much More

If your trip is focused on fall foliage, there can be no better route to follow than this one, for as the leaves of the trees change from green to red, yellow, and orange, you can follow the line of frost and the magic of a countryside in vivid color.

This is New England at its best. This is not the New England where great events of history shaped the founding of the Colonies or the New England where you walk the beach and squiggle your toes in the sand, dodging the breaking waves. This is the heart of the New England states where farmers grew their crops, where school was in one room, where the inns usually had a pub, and where having a meal at the place you slept was customary.

Suggested Pacing: Allow five nights to complete this itinerary, four if you do not cross over the Green Mountains but continue up Route 7. Spend the first night in the northwest corner of Connecticut in New Preston, Salisbury, or Norfolk then the following day continue north across the border into Massachusetts, luxuriating in the beauty of the Berkshires. Settle for the night in Stockbridge or Lenox. Continue north to Williamstown and then into Vermont to overnight in Manchester, Manchester Center, or Dorset. Cross over the Green Mountains and visit the towns of Newfane, Townshend, and West Townshend. Plan to spend the night in one of these towns where there's an inn that is certain to appeal to you. On day five conclude this itinerary either by driving north and east to Woodstock or to Shelburne, with its wonderful museum.

It's important to realize that number of miles to be driven during any one of these days is not great—to emphasize the point they are noted below (all approximate):

Norwalk to Salisbury—70
Salisbury to Stockbridge—30
Stockbridge to Manchester Center—70
Manchester Center to Townshend—40
Townshend to Woodstock—65
Townshend to Shelburne—160

This itinerary has no prescribed "sightseeing" or pace: rather it affords the "experience" of New England. You set the specifics. You can decide to meander along at a leisurely pace—pause in front of the post office and walk through the village; look at the plaque that dates a home; go into the local drug store where, if you are lucky, there will be a row of counter stools to sit and have an ice cream soda. Wander into the antique stores for the experience of seeing your grandmother's pitcher or the old kitchen spatula. Buy a postcard to send to a friend, a gift for a loved one, or a memento to take home.

Join Route 7 at its southernmost point in **Norwalk**, Connecticut. If you have just completed the itinerary that ends in the Connecticut River Valley, it will take no more than two hours to reach Norwalk and to begin the route north. If shopping in an upscale suburban community is what you feel like during the morning, go to **New Canaan** on Route 106 and visit galleries, antique stores, and other high-end shopping. New Canaan is the home of the **Silvermine Guild of Artists** with studios for studying and creating many different forms of art. Every May and June the Guild exhibits works by its members. Taking Route 106 from New Canaan back to Route 7 will put you on the path to Ridgefield, which will be the second detour—and you've hardly begun! **Ridgefield** is only an hour north of New York but you would never know it from the rural character of this lovely town. Old trees line the streets and front the gracious homes, many of which date back to the 18th and early 19th centuries. Here you will find the **Aldrich Museum of Contemporary Art** where changing exhibits display the work of today's contemporary artists.

Back on Route 7 proceed north through Danbury and above New Milford take Route 202 to **Litchfield**. With its village green and surrounding homes dating back to the 18th century, there is no prettier town in all of Connecticut. The **Litchfield First Congregational Church** is an architectural treasure, and if you are traveling here in the autumn, the church framed by the seasonal color of the trees will be one of your most memorable photographs. Return north on Route 63 to South Canaan and Canaan then drive west on Route 44 to **Salisbury**. This is yet another charmer and a great place to find an inn for the night.

The Berkshires

Cross into Massachusetts and in the towns of **Ashley Falls**, **Sheffield**, and **Great Barrington** you find a bounty of antique-shops. Referring to a local guide, available in most of these shops in the Route 7 area, will enable you to concentrate on those stores most likely to have the treasure missing from your collection. If you're not an antique lover, enjoy the towns—stop and wander about, have coffee or a bite to eat at one of the local eateries, and just absorb the charm. Ashley Falls is tiny, Sheffield is mid-size, and Great Barrington tends to be the "papa bear" of these three and the convenient center with the hardware store and the larger supermarkets.

Just 7 miles north of Great Barrington is **Stockbridge**, that grand old dame of the Berkshires. Whether you stay here or in one of the surrounding towns matters not, for there is much to do in this area. The village of Stockbridge, with its broad Main Street, lovely old trees, and one beautiful old home after another, is worth a full day. At the top of the list is a visit to the **Norman Rockwell Museum**, which houses the largest collection of the work of this famous American artist. Many pieces were used on the covers of the *Saturday Evening Post* and his depiction of everyday life rings not only true but also close to home with any viewer. Smiles are difficult to repress! In a totally different vein is **Chesterwood**, the estate of Daniel Chester French, the creator of the monument to the Minutemen in Concord, Massachusetts and, more importantly, the sculpture of Abraham Lincoln in Washington, D.C. If you want to enjoy the music of the Boston Symphony Orchestra at the **Tanglewood Music Festival**, held each summer since the 1930s, then you need to make plans to extend your stay. There are several halls in which these musical events take place, but there is nothing like sitting on the lawn with a picnic supper and a bottle of wine for a relaxing summer evening enjoying beautiful music. This is an experience not to be missed. Also in this area are the **Jacob's Pillow Dance Festival**, the **South Mountain Concert Festival**, and summer theatre at the **Berkshire Playhouse** in Stockbridge. The **Williamstown Theatre** is a little more than 30 miles to the north, also on Route 7.

Head north toward the border of Massachusetts and Vermont. Along the way plan to visit the **Hancock Shaker Village**, located outside of **Pittsfield**, and then one of my all-time favorites, the **Sterling and Francine Clark Institute** in **Williamstown**. This treasure, built by its donors in a town far away from urban centers that might be threatened by war, has collections ranging from the Renaissance to the great American painters of the 19th and 20th centuries. There are also displays of furniture and porcelain and, my particular favorite, a collection of English and American silver. Do find the time for this visit for it's an extraordinary one—a major museum in a spectacular countryside setting.

Leaving Williamstown, cross into Vermont and head for **Old Bennington**, a charming village dating back to the 18th century and steeped in Colonial history, that lies 9 miles to the west of the commercial town of **Bennington** on Route 9. Allow time for the walking tour (maps available at the Chamber of Commerce) including the **Old First Church**, the **Bennington Battle Monument**, and the **Grandma Moses Schoolhouse**, where you can see several paintings of the well-known artist who started painting at the age of 70 and continued in this career until she was 101. As a fan of folk art, I find that the primitive-style paintings of Grandma Moses with their naïve renderings of farm and country life (particularly those in winter) to be extraordinarily charming.

Continuing north on Route 7 brings you into the town of **Arlington**. At that point take Route 7A towards Manchester and Manchester Center, detouring for a short sidetrip along the scenic Equinox Skyline Drive, a 5½-mile drive to the top of **Mount Equinox** and the highest point in the Taconic Range. Views from the summit are especially wonderful in the fall when the foliage is at its best. **Manchester** and **Manchester Center** have lovely old homes sitting along their main streets, while in Manchester Center there is now a grand array of brand-name outlet shops. From Manchester Center follow Route 30 for 8 miles into **Dorset**, a favorite of mine—a small village with lovely white clapboard homes, church, and village green. Whether you're visiting in winter with the town dressed in white, in summer with the fragrance of freshly mown grass in the air and the Dorset Playhouse presenting an array of summer theatre, or in fall when frost coats the pumpkins and turns the leaves into magical colors, you're in for a special treat when you visit Dorset.

Leaving Dorset, you pass through more of the same bucolic countryside—farms and fields, rolling hills and valleys, rushing streams, sturdy stone walls, and towering trees—a photographer's paradise at any time of the year. Take Route 11 to Londonderry and turn south on Route 100 to **Jamaica**, **West Townshend**, **Townshend** and on to **Newfane**. Retrace your steps back to Townshend and head north to **Grafton**, **Chester** and **Ludlow**. This is a winding and relatively narrow route that will enhance your appreciation of the special, unique qualities of Vermont villages. The **Green Mountains** are home to some of New England's oldest and most famous ski areas—many a youngster has learned ski technique here. Each mountain has its own distinctive style of skiing and those who ski often will have a favorite. Studying the individual ski area descriptions of elevation, number of trails, degree of difficulty, and overall size should make a decision easier as to which to visit. As always, the mid-week package lift ticket is the most economical way to enjoy skiing on any mountain. Don't count these areas out at other times of the year: many of them run their ski lifts for visitors in the fall when the foliage can be enjoyed from a unique perspective on high.

Route 7 & Much More

From Ludlow you can easily conclude this itinerary in **Woodstock** by driving north on Route 100 to West Bridgewater then turning east on Route 4. Ever since the 18th century Woodstock has been a magnet for merchants, professionals, and those who wish to live in a sophisticated community. The homes, of many architectural styles, are a legacy of those prosperous citizens. Today this village is not only the commercial center for this area of Vermont, but also provides upscale shopping in its many stores and galleries.

However, if you are staying with this itinerary, turn west from Ludlow to Route 7 following it north towards **Burlington** on Lake Champlain and detouring along the way to visit **Mendon**, **Chittenden**, and **Goshen** before arriving in **Shelburne**. Be sure to visit the **Shelburne Museum** in which is displayed an incredible collection of folk art, and the crafts, furnishings, art, and tools of the trade used in the early years of the 20th century. The complex consists of 37 buildings on a 45-acre setting that is open from late May to late October. A visit to this museum is all but a must if you can add this extra day to your itinerary. There is the Circus Parade Building, the Shelburne Railroad Station, the *Ticonderoga* (a side-wheeler steamship), the Stencil House displaying decorative wall stenciling, the Colchester Reef Lighthouse with its collection of marine art, the Stagecoach Inn, and the Electra Havemeyer Webb Memorial Building with a re-creation of rooms from the Webbs' Park Avenue apartment. With this small sampling of the contents of the Shelburne Museum, you can see that it would be easy to spend more than one day exploring even a portion of what's here for your enjoyment. You can either overnight in the Shelburne area or nearby **Warren** or **Waitsfield**.

This itinerary ends here but if your travel time permits, consider continuing to the east and spending time in New Hampshire.

46

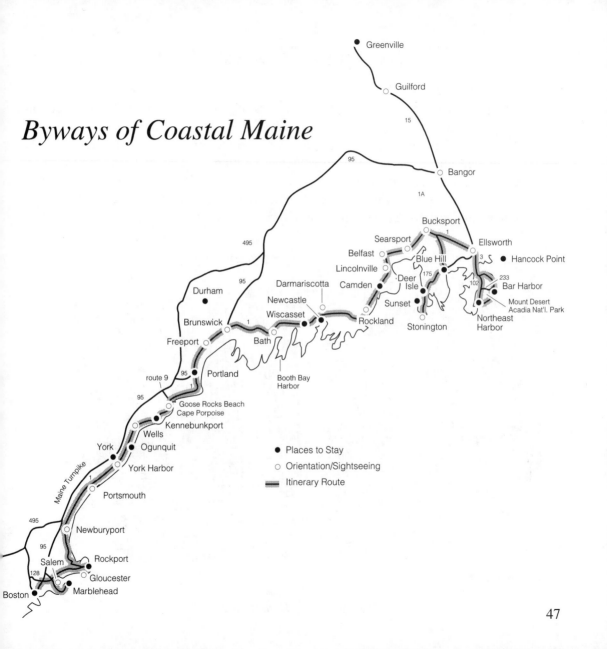

Byways of Coastal Maine

Greenville

Guilford

15

95

Bangor

1A

Buksport

Searsport

Belfast

Blue Hill

Ellsworth

3

Hancock Point

495

Lincolnville

Camden

Deer Isle

175

102

233

Bar Harbor

95

Darmariscotta

Newcastle

Wiscasset

Sunset

Mount Desert
Acadia Nat'l. Park

Durham

Brunswick

1

Rockland

Stonington

Northeast
Harbor

Freeport

Bath

route 9

95

Portland

Booth Bay
Harbor

1

95

1

Goose Rocks Beach
Cape Porpoise

York

Kennebunkport

Wells

Ogunquit

York Harbor

Portsmouth

Maine Turnpike

7

● Places to Stay

○ Orientation/Sightseeing

▨▨▨ Itinerary Route

495

Newburyport

95

Salem

Rockport

128

Gloucester

Boston

Marblehead

The Byways of Coastal Maine

There are many wonderful itineraries in New England and none is more different from the rest than the trip up the coast of Maine with its rugged beauty and picturesque charm. In the lower portions of the coast the seaside villages are all relatively near the road, while above Portland the geology of the Ice Age created long fingers into the sea as the ice retreated and you have to travel miles down winding backcountry roads to reach the tips of some peninsulas. What makes this itinerary so special is the fact that your pace is by necessity very leisurely since the roads wind from one lovely town or harbor to the next. You couldn't drive fast if you wanted to—and, believe me, you won't want to.

Marblehead Harbor

Magnificent old trees sit beside the roads with their branches hanging over the passing vehicles; houses are white and old barns have mellowed with the weather to soft browns and grays; and everywhere there are views down saltwater inlets, views that change with the rise and fall of the ocean tides.

However, before you reach this magical coast of Maine, you take the time to visit Salem and Marblehead where history buffs will find much to enjoy while walking the streets and learning about the lives of the citizens who lived in these communities over two centuries ago. Rockport and Gloucester offer visitors the opportunity to see the arts, antiques, and scenic harbors that make this part of Cape Ann so charming.

Recommended Pacing: There is no perfect way to follow this itinerary since where you spend your time will be dictated by your personal interests. Allow a minimum of six nights, five if you do not visit Salem and Marblehead. If you choose to visit Salem and Marblehead spend your first overnight here. Day two takes you to Rockport and Gloucester and the small villages in the northeastern part of Massachusetts before you cross into New Hampshire and quickly cross over the Merrimack River into Maine where you stay overnight in the area of York or Kennebunkport. Continue north through Portland and Bath to the lovely village of Wiscasset and spend the night there. The following day your drive takes you through Rockland to Camden, one of my favorite spots on the Maine coast and one of the most charming towns in which to spend the night. Conclude your itinerary in Bar Harbor with a two-night stay there to allow time to explore the Acadia National Park.

Leave Boston on I-93 north, turning onto the circumferential Route 128 and I-95. Shortly after you have turned east on I-95 and are headed towards the north shore of Massachusetts you find signs that will take you, via Route 114, towards Salem and Marblehead.

Salem, famous in the late 17th century for witchcraft hysteria, is well known now as the home of the **Peabody Essex Museum**, a superlative museum where you can easily spend several hours viewing the exhibits on the maritime history of the Massachusetts Bay

Colony. The focus is on objects collected by the ship captains of Salem on their voyages delivering the colony's goods to the capitols of Europe and Asia. Of particular note is the Asian export art collection (decorative art made in Asia for export to the West), considered to be the most complete of any in the world, which features 17th- through 19th-century decorative and utilitarian objects used in homes and businesses. There is also a great collection of maritime art, as well as a focus on Asian, Oceanic, and African art and Native American arts and archaeology. The **Witch Museum** offers exhibits and a sound and light show with vignettes of the witch trials of 1692. **Chestnut Street** is lined with mansions built by ship captains that reflect the wealth of that era and in particular of those associated with the shipping trade. Salem is also famous as the home of the **House of Seven Gables** where tours bring to life the scenes from Hawthorne's famous novel of the same name. **Pioneer Village** (open from May through October) is a re-creation of buildings that existed in the early days of the settlement of Salem. There are houses with thatched roofs, dugouts, and a wigwam. Interpreters dressed in costume explain the daily life of Salem's early settlers.

A visit to the North Shore would not be complete without a drive to **Marblehead** and a walk in the historic district dating back to the 17th and 18th centuries when Marblehead's harbor was, as it is today, a hive of activity. In fact, Marblehead is known as the sailing capitol of New England. On summer weekends, from many vantage points, you can see sailing yachts of every size and description racing and cruising among the waters of the harbor and the nearby ocean.

If you've spent the night in the Salem and Marblehead area, you'll now be facing the choice of a second day on the North Shore or moving onward into Maine. I recommend that you drive to **Gloucester** to visit **Beauport**, the **Cape Ann Historical Museum**, and, if time permits, the **Hammond Castle Museum**. My favorite of these three is Beauport, the 40-room home designed and decorated by Henry Davis Sleeper. Beauport is open from May to September and guided one-hour tours are available. If decor is of interest to you, this visit would be one you'll never forget. This is one of the many fine houses that are owned by the **SPNEA** (Society for the Preservation of New England Antiquities) and a tour of several of these properties throughout New England would be well worth an itinerary all of its own. For details contact SPNEA at (617) 227-3956 or visit their website at *www.spnea.com*.

After you leave Gloucester take Route 127A to **Rockport**. This part of **Cape Ann** is the site of an artists' colony and its galleries and surrounding shops are very busy during the summer months as visitors enjoy the scenery of the old fishing village and harbor. In the harbor one scene of an old fishing building and wharf has become so famous that it is known as "Motif # 1" to artists around the world.

Leaving the Cape Ann peninsula on Route 133, you drive through the town of **Essex**, famous for its several antique shops where you may find some treasure to take home. Route 133 connects to Route 1A through the town of Rowley and onto **Newburyport** with its magnificent High Street, once again another town made famous by its shipping history and the homes of those associated with that very prosperous trade.

Exit the Maine Turnpike (I-95, the fast interstate highway) onto Route 1 (the road that connects one old historical town to the next) as soon as you can—the exit from the turnpike in York is a perfect place to begin this journey. In this lower part of Maine you will find yourself less than a mile from the coast so driving in and out of the little coastal villages is quick and easy. If you can begin this itinerary in Maine with a drive through **York** and **York Harbor**, it's a nice way to start to relax and see the sights, and experience the sounds and smell of the ocean. There are a number of **antique shops** all along Route 1. Lower Maine has several collectives (where several dealers, rather than one, display their merchandise) in the York area.

Continuing north from the Yorks brings you to **Ogunquit**, which, in the language of the American Indian tribe of the Algonquins, means "beautiful place by the sea." The long, narrow harbor is especially scenic and while you may not see the lobster boats depart early in the morning, you can catch them returning in the afternoon with a following of inquisitive sea gulls seeking a free dinner. Because of the attractiveness of this area, many artists settled here—the subjects for their art are everywhere. The Ogunquit Playhouse offers theatre performances on summer evenings.

Traffic along Route 1 as you drive north to Wells can be especially tedious—even more so on a foggy or rainy day when all the tourists are searching for entertainment and are visiting the concentration of outlet shops at the southern end of this route. I'd suggest, if possible, avoiding this drive at the beginning or the end of the beach day, when those who have spent the day on the sand and in the ocean find their way to restaurants, grocery stores, and back to their overnight accommodations.

In the town of **Wells** there's a real concentration of antique shops offering formal and country furniture and decorative objects. Just north of Wells, Route 9 breaks off to the town of **Kennebunkport** and I strongly recommend that you drive into "the Port," as the locals call it. This is a storybook village, with an origin as a fishing port. You can still see the lobstermen go out to sea each day to empty their traps and to bait them for the next day's catch. Kennebunkport has become a tourist mecca, especially in respect to its shops. To absorb the charm of this town with its lovely stately homes and elm-tree-lined streets, allow time to include a walking tour of the town center. Afterwards, find a spot to have a cup of New England clam chowder or a Maine lobster. One of the sights outside the town is the **Wedding Cake House** on Route 9A, which, as the stories go, was decorated with all manner of gingerbread trim by a sea captain who was called to sea immediately after his wedding.

Just north of Kennebunkport, taking Ocean Avenue first east and then north from the village, you come to the **summer home** of the 41st president of the United States, **George Bush**. Shortly thereafter along Route 9, you reach **Cape Porpoise**, which exudes all the charm of a tiny fishing community with houses set on hills looking down on its lobster boats and other small craft. It's tiny and will take only a short time to visit, but it's charming. Back on Route 9 you continue north a few miles to a barn on your left with a clock tower and a somewhat indecisive sign on your right that points to the beach called **Goose Rocks**. With its one tiny store, this beach is a magnificent 2-mile-long stretch of sand—a rarity on the rocky coast of Maine. If you're able to linger here you become immediately aware that the tides on this northeast coast rise and fall 10 feet or more with each change of tide, so that the beach you walk at low tide will become much narrower as the tide comes in. If you put a toe into the water, you quickly learn that swimming on the coast of Maine takes a degree of courage!

Portland Head Light

From Goose Rocks drive north on Route 9 to Route 1 north and then take I-95 onward to Portland. The city of **Portland**, with its population of about 65,000, is the largest town you come to as you go northward along the coast. The port is an important one for the fishing industry and the city has become the center for commercial business in northern New England. This is a city that is perfect for sightseeing on foot since all the interesting spots are within a short distance of one another. There is also an advantage to walking as the pace allows you to study the architecture and permits the occasional glimpse into a hidden garden here and there. Portland has a great historical area and is a regional center for the arts. The **Museum of Art** focuses on artists of the state of Maine and there are wonderful paintings by Winslow Homer, Andrew Wyeth, Edward Hopper, and John Marin. For those interested in seeing more of **Casco Bay**, there are seasonal daily trips by boat to view the islands, though it is not always possible to disembark.

From Portland you can take a ferry to Nova Scotia but unless your time is very limited, I suggest you continue a little farther north by car along the coast to Bar Harbor. This is well worth the time, and from there it is a much shorter sea trip to reach the maritime provinces.

About 12 miles northeast of Portland on the I-95 is the town of **Freeport**, made famous by the **L. L. Bean store**, open 24 hours a day. Here you can find everything from a canoe to a camp stove to a ski cap and now this famous institution has expanded into selling almost anything you can use in your home. Freeport has also become home to more than 120 brand-name outlet stores of every type, so, if shopping is your thing, this is the place to "shop till you drop." Of greater interest to me than the outlet shops is the **Desert of Maine**, a phenomenon of former forest where the winds of time have laid bare more than 500 acres of sand, now formed into sand dunes—in an area nowhere near the sea. To reach and view this phenomenon (open from early May until mid-October), take I-95 to exit 19 and then drive 2 miles west on Desert Road.

North of Freeport is the community of **Brunswick**, home of **Bowdoin College** and the **Bowdoin College Museum of Art** with its collections of early-American portraits and, annually from mid-May until mid-August, a display of the paintings, etchings, and memorabilia of the artist Winslow Homer. The particular focus of much of his work was the coast and lore of Maine, so this becomes a topical experience for those interested in the work of this very famous American artist.

Just north of Brunswick, Route 1 begins its coastal-hugging path toward Bar Harbor, still 150 miles to the north. Long fingers of land stretch out into the sea and a trip down any of these will bring great pleasure as you meander along winding, tree-lined roads between one small fishing village and the next. The village of **Bath** has been a shipbuilding center for hundreds of years, and its harbor hosts the relics of schooners from long ago. You can see ships in dry dock being repaired, in mothballs, or in the process of being built. As you view the wide harbor, it's easy to imagine a time when commercial ships sailed from this port to the European capitols, to the Far East, and to the West Indies. In Bath a visit to the **Maine Maritime Museum**, with its exhibits on coastal life, the shipbuilding industry, and the commerce of Maine, would provide an interesting diversion for both adults and children. There is a movie on the lobstering industry as well as exhibits in a sail loft. During the summer you can take a boat ride on the **Kennebec River** to observe the boat-building industry as it exists today.

Proceed north across the bridge to the town of **Wiscasset**, one of my very favorite villages in all of New England—I especially love its long street leading down to the water. This is another community with tree-lined streets, white churches, and lovely old homes dating back to the 18th century. It's also a terrific and popular center for antiquing, with an emphasis on country things rather than formal. In the winter the pace is slower with the fickle weather and some dealers open and others not, both adding to the charm of a visit when you find a treasure that has just been acquired by the antique dealer.

Beyond Wiscasset you are now in one of the most famous of all Maine regions—**Boothbay Harbor**. With a year-round population of only a couple of thousand, this is an area that can absorb the summer residents, the visitors staying the night, and those who will simply be passing through on the way north or south. Charm is at every bend in the road as one scenic vista opens onto yet another and as one lovely old farmhouse with attached great barn and old faded color siding leads to the next. Extraordinarily special are the little inlets from the sea with water shimmering so brightly that it almost blinds the eye and wonderfully green trees lining the banks. These saltwater  extensions of the ocean bring the sights, sounds, and smells right up to the highway. With a dock here and there and a boat tied up, perhaps with a morning check of the lobster pots, this is a scene that will bring out your camera to capture a delightful memory. From the early spring green of new leaves signaling the end of winter, through the summer grasses and the multi-colored wildflowers, to the colors of fall, this is Maine at its best. Add the flavors of the seafood from the neighboring waters, especially lobster served boiled or stuffed, cold or hot with melted butter, and your visit is something special.

While I was visiting not only did I have my fair share of lobster in every form, but also I enjoyed the seasonal, local clams, oysters, and Maine shrimp.

If you are interested in islands and the charm they provide, you can take a boat trip from Boothbay Harbor, New Harbor, or Port Clyde to **Mohegan Island**. Lobstering is the island's principal trade, and the large number of artists who spend the summer here and work in the area augments the island's population. There are miles of trails for the hiker and spectacular views from practically every vantage point. Any photographer would find that a visit here provides more subject matter than there is film.

Working your way north again along Route 1, you will come upon **Newcastle** and, just north of it, **Damariscotta**. Both are seafaring villages with restaurants, shops, and overnight accommodations. Everything's informal here and you find the down-east Maine resident to be as special in his accent as in his friendliness.

Rockland, with its almost 8,000 population, is the next town of size. It has all the hustle and bustle and commercial activity of a modern seaport from which lobsters are shipped throughout the world. Here you find the **Farnsworth Art Museum**, which is almost a required stop because of its 19th- and 20th-century paintings by Fitzhugh Lane and a large collection of paintings by members of the Wyeth family, who traditionally summered in Maine. Their ability to capture local Maine scenery and everyday events in oil and watercolor makes a visit to this museum a rewarding experience.

Farther north on Route 1 is another of my favorite towns on the Maine coast—**Camden**, which surrounds a protected harbor full of windjammer schooners moored on summer weekends, as well as gorgeous yachts cruising the waters of **Penobscot Bay**. This is a harbor of constant activity—a photographer's dream from any angle. At the head of the harbor high on the hill is the **Camden Library** and from its windows and terraces there are unforgettable views of all that lies below. **Main Street**, lined with white mansions and yet more New England churches, is a great place to stop for lunch if your meandering around the town has you there at that hour. Enjoy the lovely architecture of the homes around you. There are art galleries, shops, and restaurants and in summer, windowboxes and flowers thrive in the day's sun and the evening's cool temperatures. It would be difficult to think of a nicer place to stay than this delightful town. There is a good little walking guide available locally, which I urge you to follow, for it will greatly enhance your visit to Camden.

Leaving Camden, travel northward along the coast through the towns of Belfast, Searsport, and Bucksport. Time should permit a drive down into the **Blue Hill Peninsula** to **Deer Isle, Sunset**, and the incredible harbor of **Stonington**, one of the most photographed harbors anywhere.

There's no way to return to the highway without taking another country road but the Blue Hill Peninsula is wide enough to allow a different view from its eastern side. After the town of Ellsworth you leave Route 1, taking Route 3 down into Mount Desert Island and the **Acadia National Park**. This park is an unforgettable experience and will cap your trip on the Maine coast: it is well worth the effort of getting there. Plan on at least one overnight in this area if you intend to spend any time in the Acadia National Park (we have inn recommendations in Bar Harbor and Northeast Harbor). The smallness and compactness of this area allows for easy visiting of all that there is to do.

Mount Desert Island is about 108 square miles in size, its beauty lying in its granite quarries, mountains, pine forests, and freshwater lakes. From high on top of any of its mountains are panoramic views over the park and the surrounding islands. There are rocky mountains with exposed granite and charming plants that seem determined to make the most of a short-lived season. Bright and diminutive wildflowers, low, scrubby blueberries, and plants with colorful leaves and berries will charm your camera with yet another photo opportunity. You can tour the park by car, guided bus, bicycle, or horse and carriage. You will want to linger and stop often, so I urge you to arm yourself with informational materials available at the National Park Headquarters and head off on your own.

Be sure to find and follow **Loop Road**, the park's main attraction, as it winds its way along the coast and up to Cadillac Mountain. There are many places to park and to gaze, to photograph and to smell, and birds to watch in this ever-changing landscape. Be sure to get to the top of **Cadillac Mountain** for the spectacular views (and take a windbreaker with you to protect you from the chilly breezes.) Other points of interest include **Otter Cliffs** and **Thunder Hole**—the water rushing into this narrow cavern with the changing tide sounds like thunder. If you have time, be sure to walk the **Beach Cliff Trail** and visit **Bass Head Light** and other areas of the national park located in the **Schoodic Peninsula**.

Mount Desert Coastline

A visit to the village of **Bar Harbor** is more enjoyable in the summer when you will find it alive with activity and summer residents—in the winter many of its shops are closed. However, in the winter the pace is slower and there is a special, quiet charm without the crowds. In the late 19th and early 20th centuries Bar Harbor became a fashionable alternative to Newport, Rhode Island. Summer homes are grand beyond your wildest imagination and driving around Bar Harbor and down to either **Northeast Harbor** or **Southwest Harbor** will take you back to another era.

This itinerary ends at Bar Harbor, which is also the beginning of other journeys onward to Nova Scotia by boat and into the upper reaches of Maine and the Moosehead Lake region on the way to Quebec. There is no doubt that a visit to **Greenville** and a stay there would provide the traveler with unique experiences. Where else can you stay in one locale and go dog sledding, ice fishing, whitewater rafting, snowmobiling, cross-country or downhill skiing, participate in a moose safari, and have a guide instruct you in the fine art of fly fishing? Seaplanes are a popular mode of transportation in these northern parts but if you're driving in the back woods on unpaved roads, a four-wheel-drive vehicle is good insurance that you'll arrive at your destination. I stayed on the main roads and had no problems at all.

By heading west from Bar Harbor you can take an alternative route across Maine into New Hampshire and Vermont, visiting the more northern areas of the **White and Green Mountains**. Herein lie small New England towns where farming and milk production are the principal industries, and where being off the beaten track is not an inconvenience, but rather a wonderful bonus. These small New England towns truly paint a picture and provide a poetic sense of New England and there is much joy in finding an inn with a cozy fireplace, a nice dining room, and congenial hosts.

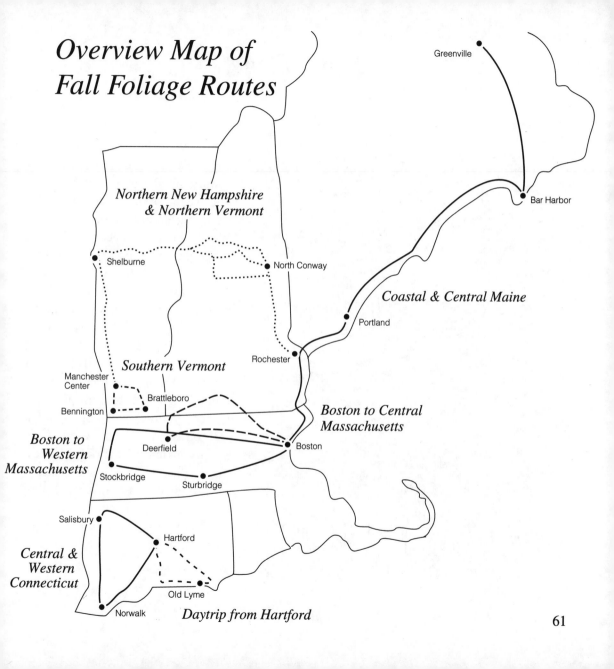

*Overview Map of
Fall Foliage Routes*

Greenville

Bar Harbor

*Northern New Hampshire
& Northern Vermont*

Shelburne

North Conway

Coastal & Central Maine

Portland

Rochester

Southern Vermont

Manchester
Center

Brattleboro

Bennington

*Boston to Central
Massachusetts*

Deerfield

Boston

*Boston to
Western
Massachusetts*

Stockbridge

Sturbridge

Salisbury

Hartford

*Central &
Western
Connecticut*

Old Lyme

Norwalk

Daytrip from Hartford

61

Fall Foliage

While New England is special at any time of the year, there is simply nowhere on earth where you can experience nature's changing colors as you can here. When the days become shorter, the nights turn cool, the first frost coats the lawn, and the roof shingles sparkle with their early-morning ice, New England prepares for the magic season of fall foliage. Trees and shrubs, flowers and weeds all begin a transformation that changes their color from green to multiple hues of red, yellow, and gold—and a million shades in between. It is simply a time of magic! And it's also the time when nature performs with a brilliant display reminiscent of fireworks on the fourth of July. It is a time to be in New England.

Devil's Hopyard

Fall Foliage

Fall foliage is generally at its peak in the first two weeks of October after the first bite of cold temperatures and seems to be best when there has been the proper amount of rainfall during the spring and summer. This season of changing colors generally begins in the far northern reaches of New England (unless you happen to be on a winding lane in the Connecticut valley alongside a quiet pond where the cold air of the night has settled in and painted everything in sight with a vivid brush of intensity). The turning of the colors generally wends its way southward, unless it happens to turn west or unless you happen to be on the peak of a mountain enjoying views for miles around. Remember, each rule about the timing of fall foliage has an exception.

This special time in New England, unless the weather is unusual, will perform as it has for hundreds of years. Do not worry excessively, or perhaps at all, about being on exactly the perfect road at the precise moment when the foliage achieves its peak and the golden and red leaves fall from the trees. Generally, plan to be in New England between mid-September and mid-October—farther north in the middle of September, and in Massachusetts and Connecticut in the month of October.

In the following pages we outline by state seven driving routes that weave through some gorgeous regions where the richness of your day will be matched not only by the color of the foliage but by each passing farm with pumpkins and gourds piled high and corn stalks tied to fence posts. Study the overview map and choose one that suits your location and time frame. These fall foliage itineraries can be followed at other times of the year, too, for they are picturesque routes to follow and great towns to visit in any season.

Reservations: The northeast's fall foliage is without any doubt one of the most popular tourist attractions in the U.S. and finding places to spend the night is sometimes difficult, so reservations are a must. Hopefully, you'll be able to find a place to suit your preference among the inns recommended in this guide. If there is no room available, ask the innkeeper for his or her recommendation of an alternative accommodation—most innkeepers recommend only places that they themselves would stay, so you'll be safe with their suggestions. Nonetheless, making a reservation as soon as you book your airplane ticket or decide to take off in your car is well advised.

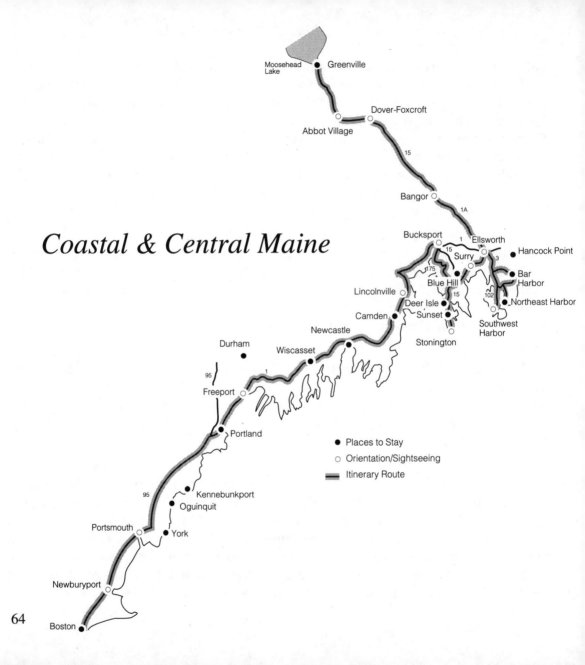

Coastal & Central Maine

- Moosehead Lake
- Greenville
- Dover-Foxcroft
- Abbot Village
- 15
- Bangor
- 1A
- Bucksport
- 1
- Ellsworth
- 15
- Surry
- Hancock Point
- 175
- 3
- Blue Hill
- Bar Harbor
- Lincolnville
- 15
- Deer Isle
- 102
- Camden
- Sunset
- Northeast Harbor
- Newcastle
- Stonington
- Southwest Harbor
- Durham
- Wiscasset
- 95
- 1
- Freeport
- Portland
- 95
- Kennebunkport
- Oguinquit
- Portsmouth
- York
- Newburyport
- Boston

- ● Places to Stay
- ○ Orientation/Sightseeing
- ▬ Itinerary Route

Coastal & Central Maine

Recommended Pacing: Three nights should do the trick, with a night in Wiscasset or Camden, followed by two in Bar Harbor. If you have time, extend your trip to stay in Greenville.

This itinerary begins 25 miles north of Portland where you exit the I-95 at **Brunswick** for a leisurely drive along Route 1 into the gorgeous village of **Wiscasset**. Continuing on Route 1, you arrive in **Camden**, a pretty town with mesmerizing views of the harbor and coastal schooners. The trip down to the **Blue Hill Peninsula** is a drive I'd recommend at any time of year and certainly in the fall with the foliage and the warm days and cool nights. From Route 1 take Route 175 south at **Bucksport** and then Route 15 to **Deer Isle** and **Stonington** where you turn north on Route 175 to the charming village of **Blue Hill** and then follow Route 172 to **Surry** and **Ellsworth**. If time permits, continue down Route 3 from Ellsworth to Route 102 to **Southwest Harbor** and then, turning north, take Route 196 to **Northeast Harbor** and then Route 3 for an overnight in Bar Harbor. If you've never visited **Bar Harbor** and the **Acadia National Park**, do plan to do so while you're here. I recommend that you allow two days for exploring the Blue Hill Peninsula and Mount Desert Island, adding to this if you intend to visit the national park with its gorgeous scenery. See *The Byways of Coastal Maine* for more detailed sightseeing information on this lovely area.

Our itinerary ends here but if you have a love of remoter places, extend your stay in Maine to visit Greenville. Leave Bar Harbor, taking Route 1A to **Bangor,** Route 15 north to **Dover,** and Route 16 west to **Abbot Village**. Here you pick up Route 15 north to **Greenville** and **Moosehead Lake**. Central Maine is many long miles connected by towns that are few and somewhat far between and well off the beaten path. It's a long drive but the reward is great. From the hills overlooking Moosehead Lake, the views are spectacular and the shimmering surface of the water seems to enhance all that surrounds it. The Bar Harbor to Greenville trip took me about three hours, allowing for one antique store where I made several purchases.

Northern New Hampshire & Northern Vermont

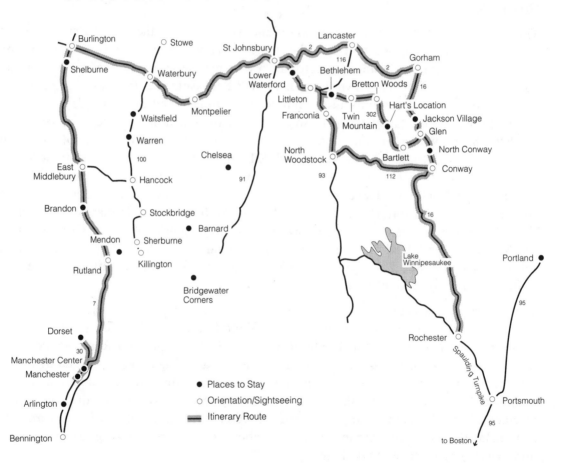

Burlington
Stowe
St Johnsbury
Lancaster
116
2
Gorham
Shelburne
Waterbury
Lower
Waterford
Bethlehem
2
16
Bretton Woods
Montpelier
Littleton
Hart's Location
Waitsfield
Franconia
302
Jackson Village
Twin
Mountain
Glen
Warren
100
Chelsea
North
Woodstock
Bartlett
North Conway
East
Middlebury
Hancock
91
93
112
Conway
Brandon
Stockbridge
16
Mendon
Barnard
Sherburne
Rutland
Killington
Lake
Winnipesaukee
Portland
7
Bridgewater
Corners
95
Dorset
30
Manchester Center
Rochester
Manchester
Portsmouth
Arlington
95
Bennington
to Boston

● Places to Stay
○ Orientation/Sightseeing
▓ Itinerary Route

Spaulding Turnpike

Northern New Hampshire & Northern Vermont

Recommended Pacing: Three nights will enable you to cover the entire itinerary. If you just wish to complete the eastern portion, drive through the White Mountains of New Hampshire, stay for two nights in North Conway, then leave the itinerary at St. Johnsbury and travel south on the I-91 into Massachusetts. However, if you have time, continue on to explore the Green Mountains of Vermont. Option One meanders along the western side of the Green Mountain National Forest and gives you a night in Manchester Center, Manchester, or Dorset. Option Two traces the eastern edge of the national forest to visit the charming villages of southern Vermont, giving you a night in Stockbridge or Hancock.

The fall foliage turns brilliant in the northern areas of these two states at more or less the same time, so it is logical to combine them into one tour. An hour's drive from Boston will bring you to **Rochester**, New Hampshire to start this itinerary. Continue along that very scenic route leading into **Conway** and **North Conway** and the heart of the wintertime ski area. In these mountain towns you will find a ski area or two that will be running their lifts to the top of the mountain during the fall and this is a glorious way to rise above the trees and to gaze down, at first to the areas below you, and then from the top of the mountain to the vistas of the surrounding countryside. In many instances these vistas include a blue lake lying below a swath of color, as if an artist were painting a brightly lit canvas.

From the Conways there are three routes, resembling fingers, heading into the western portion of northern New Hampshire. An excellent daytrip is to take the northern finger out of North Conway, returning back in the evening via the middle finger. The northernmost finger follows Route 16 north to **Jackson** and **Gorham**. Turn west at Gorham, to connect with Route 2 to **Lancaster**, from which point pick up Route 116 south to **Littleton** and then east through **Bethlehem**, following Route 302 through **Twin Mountain**, **Bretton Woods**, **Crawford North**, **Hart's Location**, and **Bartlett** to **Glen**. Here you pick up Route 16 south, which returns you to North Conway.

Leave Conway via the "lower finger," turning west just south of town on Route 112, known as the **Kancamagus Highway**. This road rises through the **White Mountains** and is just simply beautiful. It twists and winds, rises and falls, making every scenically beautiful mile one to remember. The road ends in **North Woodstock** and from this point you head north via the I-93 to **Franconia, Bethlehem, Lower Waterford** and **St. Johnsbury** where you can leave the itinerary to travel south into Massachusetts on the I-91 or continue on Route 2 to **Montpelier**, the capitol of Vermont. The recently remodeled state capitol building is wonderful to tour.

Option One: Travel northwest on I-89 through **Waterbury** to the commercial center of **Burlington** on Lake Champlain where you turn south on Route 7 to **Shelburne**. Be sure to visit its wonderful museum, which we cover in detail on page 45. Continue south on the 7, tracing the western edge of the **Green Mountain National Forest** to spend the night in **Manchester, Manchester Center**, or the lovely village of **Dorset**. Once again, be prepared for the growing frequency of antique shops and drivers, like me, who will brake and turn quickly to one side of the road or the other for that familiar sign beginning with the letters "ANT...."

Option Two: Travel northwest on I-89 until you reach the exit for Route 100 in **Waterbury** where you turn south on Route 100 for a narrow and winding drive along the eastern side of the **Green Mountain National Forest**. Traveling this road will be slow, but the scenery is spectacular and in many places you'll be driving along a river with periodic white water and an occasional waterfall. On this route you pass through **Waitsfield, Warren**, and **Granville** and then proceed south to **Stockbridge** to conclude the itinerary in **Sherburne**, home of the Killington ski mountain.

Southern Vermont

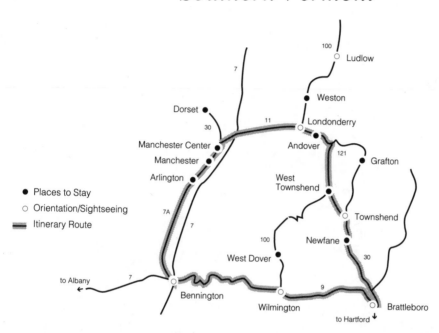

Recommended Pacing: This itinerary is a circle trip from Brattleboro with one night in the Dorset/Manchester area.

This itinerary begins in **Brattleboro** where you exit the I-91 and drive northwest on Route 30, along the eastern side of the **Green Mountain National Forest**, ambling through the towns of **Newfane**, **Townshend**, and **West Townshend**. Join Route 100 going north to **Londonderry** and west on Route 11 to **Manchester**, **Manchester Center**, and **Dorset**. Spend the night in this area then go south to **Bennington** where you have yet another fabulous drive back through the **Green Mountain National Forest** on Route 9 east to **Brattleboro**.

Boston to Central Massachusetts

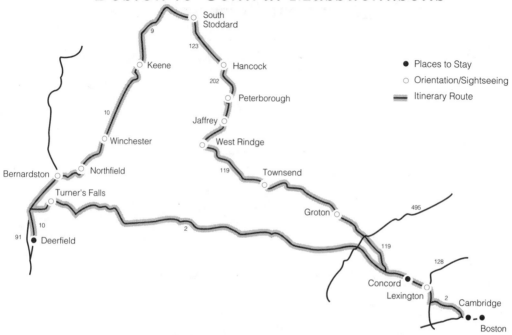

Recommended Pacing: This is a round trip from Boston spending one night in Deerfield. Leave **Boston** on Route 2 west to **Lexington** and **Concord** to visit these lovely towns and their historical sites. (See sightseeing on pages 33–34.) At the traffic circle on Route 2 after you leave Concord, take Route 2A to Route 119 to **Groton** and **Townshend**. Continue west on 119 to **West Rindge** and then turn north on Route 202 to **Jaffrey, Peterborough,** and **Hancock**. From Hancock take Route 123 west to **South Stoddard**, where you turn left on Route 9 southwest to **Keene**, New Hampshire, picking up Route 10 south to **Winchester** and **Northfield** and on to **Bernardston**. Here you take I-91 south to **Greenfield**, exiting there to take Route 10 to **Deerfield**, a delightful historical treasure. From Deerfield go north on Route 2A to **Turners Falls** and then proceed on Route 2 east back to **Boston**.

Boston to Western Massachusetts

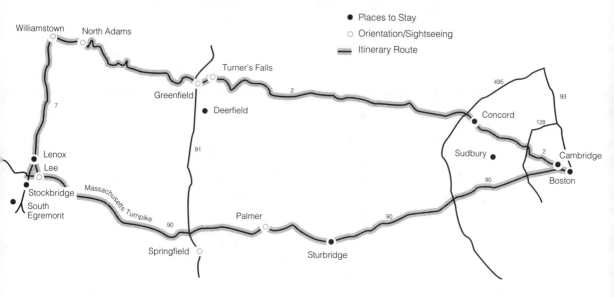

Recommended Pacing: Spend one night in Stockbridge or Lenox before returning to Boston. If you intend to spend a full day in Sturbridge Village, plan on overnighting there.

Leave **Boston** on Route 2, following it all the way to the other side of the state in **Williamstown**. (Don't even think of missing a visit to the **Sterling and Francine Clark Institute** located there.) From Williamstown, travel south on Route 7 to **Lenox**, **Stockbridge**, and **Great Barrington**. While speed is not always best, the drive on the Massachusetts Turnpike (I-90) east through **Lee** and **Springfield** and to **Palmer**, with an exit from the turnpike onto Route 20 east through the country to **Sturbridge**, will allow a visit to **Sturbridge Village**, with its demonstrations of the crafts, homes, and lifestyle of 200 years ago. This is a very special treat, with or without children. From Sturbridge take the fast route back into **Boston** on the Massachusetts Turnpike.

Central & Western Connecticut

Canaan
Salisbury
Norfolk
44
South
Canaan
New Hartford
West Cornwall
Cornwall Bridge
Avon
7
44
8
New Preston
Hartford
Kent
84
91
New Milford
84
15
91
Danbury
Waterbury
84
15
35
15
New Haven
Ridgefield
1
Wilton
Norwalk
Westport
15

● Places to Stay
○ Orientation/Sightseeing
Itinerary Route

Central & Western Connecticut

Recommended Pacing: Overnight in Salisbury, New Preston, Ridgefield, or Westport before returning to Hartford, your originating town.

Hartford, Connecticut is the perfect jumping-off point for this tour. Travel west on Route 44 from **Hartford** through **Avon**, to **New Hartford, Norfolk**, and **Canaan**. At Canaan go south on Route 7 through **South Canaan** and **West Cornwall** to **Cornwall Bridge**, continuing on through **Kent** and **New Milford** to **Danbury**.

From Danbury stay on Route 7 south, with a detour on Route 35 to see the lovely town of **Ridgefield**, getting back on Route 7 to **Wilton**. Shortly afterwards you reach the Merritt Parkway (Route 15), a highway planned and built years ago when driving was considered to be a scenic experience as well as a means of getting from one point to another.

Take the Merritt Parkway through **New Haven** back up to **Hartford**, thereby completing the loop.

Daytrip from Hartford

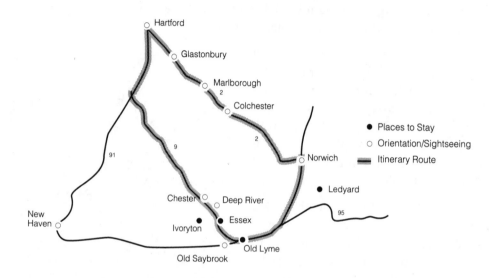

Recommended Pacing: A leisurely daytrip from Hartford.

With **Hartford** as your starting point, set out on I-91 south to Route 9 south to the towns alongside the Connecticut River: **Chester**, **Deep River**, **Essex**, **Old Saybrook**, and **Old Lyme**. I would opt for a short spurt of high speed on I-95 east (the Connecticut turnpike) to Route 85 northwest to Route 2 northwest through **Colchester**, **Marlborough**, and **Glastonbury** back to **Hartford**.

Connecticut
Places to Stay- Map 1

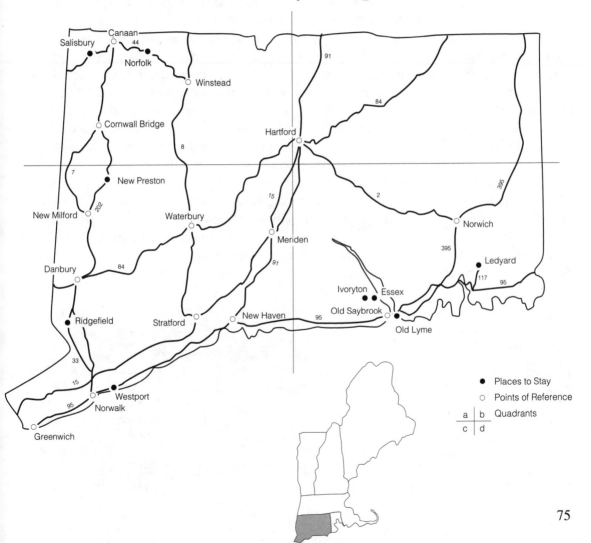

Places to Stay
Points of Reference
Quadrants

The unspoiled Connecticut River Valley, with its delightful, historic river towns founded in the 17th century, is undoubtedly one of the most scenic areas in the state. None of these towns is more charming than Essex and there is no more enchanting place to stay there than the Griswold Inn, known for its dining rooms with their collection of marine art and their inviting, cozy atmosphere which makes you linger a while, and then a little while longer. A hostelry since the day it opened in 1776, it also offers most appealing accommodations—the owners have created in each of the guestrooms a level of charm and comfort that, like the dining rooms, makes for instant relaxation. The air-conditioned, pine-floored rooms and suites, of various shapes and sizes, are located in five buildings on both sides of the street. I stayed in a long, narrow suite above two shops with a great window seat looking out into the courtyard. The first floors of these separate buildings house little gift shops where you can find that perfect gift to take home. Essex's attractions include the Connecticut River Museum, which presents the history of the valley and its maritime heritage, a steam train and riverboat ride, taking a quiet stroll along the quaint old riverfront, or just gazing at the river through your bedroom window. *Directions*: From I-91 exit at 22 south and follow Route 9 south to exit 3 for Essex and the inn. From I-95 leave at exit 69 and follow Route 9 north to exit 3.

GRISWOLD INN
Innkeepers: Joan & Doug Paul
36 Main Street
Essex, CT 06426
Tel: (860) 767-1776, Fax: (860) 767-0481
E-mail: griswoldinn@snet.net
14 rooms, 16 suites, Double: $90–$195
Open all year
Credit cards: all major
Restaurant: lunch & dinner (closed Christmas)
Handicap room
www.karenbrown.com/ne/griswoldinn.html

Originally the home of an ivory comb and keyboard manufacturer, this turn-of-the-century building is set in lovely gardens and a native woodland in the village of Ivoryton. The magnificent copper beech tree standing in front of the inn gives it its name. In the main house four guestrooms, each air-conditioned, have been beautifully restored with private baths and in the renovated Carriage House you find nine rooms with whirlpool baths, TVs, and doors leading out to private decks. I especially loved the feeling of these Carriage House rooms with their soaring ceilings and exposed original supporting beams. One of the bedrooms in the main building has flowered wallpaper, a canopied brass bed, a love seat in front of the fireplace, and a chaise lounge—a great spot for an afternoon nap. The decor in this inn is traditional but the guest has all the amenities that guarantee a restful stay. The inn's dining rooms, featuring hearty French country-style food served at tables set with linens, fresh flowers, and sparkling silver, are warm and inviting and there's a plant-filled Victorian-style conservatory offering a perfect spot for a glass of wine before dinner or an after-dinner drink. I didn't have the opportunity to dine here but the sophisticated menu, which includes patés, caviar, salmon, lobster, and pheasant, certainly promises a memorable evening of great gastronomy. *Directions:* From New Haven drive east on I-95 to exit 69, travel north on Route 9 to exit 3, then west for 1¾ miles to the inn.

COPPER BEECH INN
Innkeepers: Sally & Eldon Senner
46 Main Street
Ivoryton, CT 06442
Tel: (860) 767-0330 or (888) 809-2056, Fax: None
13 rooms, Double: $105–$180
Closed Christmas Eve & Day, first week of January
Credit cards: all major
Restaurant: breakfast, dinner (Tues. through Sun.)
Handicap accessible rooms & restaurant
www.karenbrown.com/ne/copperbeechinn.html

The Stonecroft Country Inn is located on a winding country road adjoining a nature preserve and provides the visitor with a true escape from the pace of busy times. The inn has ten bedrooms, some in the historic 19th-century house and the rest in the building that houses the inn's restaurant. Fireplaces abound and there are whirlpool tubs for your enjoyment. There's a wonderful blend of luxury and simplicity, where everything that the guest could want is right at hand. Rooms in the main house are smaller, as one would imagine in an historic structure, but they are very attractive with their New England fabrics and warm, cozy charm. In the newer building there are four rooms on the first floor and two suites on the second; these are spacious, with cathedral ceilings, canopied beds, and oversized bathrooms. When you add a first-class restaurant with a European-trained chef, this inn makes for a complete package. It takes a little bit of time to get to the surrounding attractions but the inn is so inviting that you might just stay put and enjoy the peacefulness of the surroundings. The restaurant is open by reservation only so be sure to call if you plan to dine there. *Directions:* Take I-95 to exit 89 and then turn left if coming from the south or right if coming from the north for 3¼ miles to the inn.

STONECROFT COUNTRY INN
Innkeepers: Joan & Lynn Egy
515 Pumpkin Hill Road
Ledyard, CT 06339
Tel: (860) 572-0771, Fax: (860) 572-9161
E-mail: stoncrft@concentric.net
8 rooms, 2 suites
Double: $150–$250
Open all year
Credit cards: all major
Restaurant: dinner six nights by reservation
Handicap room

Nestled in the northwestern corner of Connecticut, Boulders Inn sits perched on a hill, just under a mountain, with expansive views of Lake Waramaug. Within this wonderful building constructed of massive native stone there is an inn with a first-class restaurant. The guestrooms in the inn are furnished with a combination of country classics and antiques, while four separate guesthouses—Gem, Nugget, Fieldstone, and Cobble—are furnished in country decor and have private decks and wood-burning fireplaces. There is also a carriage house with three traditionally furnished rooms, each enjoying a stone fireplace. I loved the feel of the glass-enclosed dining room overlooking the lake and found the food, which features "new American" cuisine, most appetizing. In the summer dining is also available on the outside terraces. Activities at or nearby the inn include swimming, boating, hiking, skiing, and golf. This is a great base from which to go antiquing and attend musical and art events in the area. *Directions*: Take I-84 to exit 7 to Route 7 north to New Milford, then Route 202 to New Preston where you turn left on Route 45 to the inn.

BOULDERS INN
Innkeepers: Ulla & Kees Adema
East Shore Road, P.O. Box 2575
New Preston, CT 06777
Tel: (860) 868-0541 or (800) 552-6853
Fax: (860) 868-1925
E-mail: boulders@bouldersinn.com
6 rooms, 3 suites, 4 guesthouses
Double: $260–$380
Open all year
Credit cards: all major
Restaurant: breakfast, dinner,
 and lunch seasonally on weekends
Handicap room
www.karenbrown.com/ne/bouldersinn.html

To stay at Manor House is to visit a grand home built a century ago and as you approach the front door along the winding driveway, it's somehow easy to imagine that earlier life. When you walk through the door into the large hallway from which rises a grand staircase you're sure that you are about to experience a romantic retreat. As the surroundings begin to come into focus you're aware of incredible architectural details and then you notice the exquisite Tiffany stained-glass windows in the dining room and living room. I stopped, I stared, and I thought how wonderful it was to be a guest in this home. The comfortable guestrooms are all furnished with period antiques. I stayed in the room that was originally the master bedroom—its sitting area in front of the fireplace would have been a good place to linger longer than time permitted. Some rooms have fireplaces, some have private balconies, some have oversized Jacuzzis or soaking tubs. From the many windows views encompass lawns, gardens, and countryside. When I arrived I was welcomed by the smell of baking bread, an enticing prelude to the delicious breakfast, which includes honey from Manor House's own hives. There's an inn cat that would have spent the night on my bed had I known it was around. *Directions:* Take I-84 to the exit for Route 8 north at Waterbury. At the end of Route 8 (Winsted) take Route 44 west to Norfolk.

MANOR HOUSE
Innkeepers: Diane & Henry Tremblay
69 Maple Avenue
Norfolk, CT 06058
Tel & fax: (860) 542-5690
E-mail: tremblay@esslink.com
8 rooms, 1 suite, Double: $115–$250
Open all year
Credit cards: all major
Restaurant: none
Handicap room: none
www.karenbrown.com/ne/manorhouse.html

One of the most charming villages in Connecticut must be Old Lyme where the Bee and Thistle Inn was built as a private home in 1756. Its second owners found its location too close to the road so moved it back to its present gracious setting, adding enhancements such as the lovely sunken garden. In the late 1930s this home was transformed into an inn, now updated by the present owners to offer 11 guestrooms and a cottage. From the welcoming front hall there's a lovely carved staircase that takes you up to the tastefully decorated bedrooms on the upper floors. The rooms, with sitting areas and full bathrooms, have everything that a guest might want. Flowered wallpapers, canopy beds with fishnet coverings, quilts, and Oriental rugs all add to the charm. The inn is noted for its award-winning restaurant and the dining rooms are as attractive as the common rooms with their individual fireplaces. Candlelight adds a magical touch to the dining experience. There's a very special cottage that will give you splendid isolation in the midst of all that there is to do in this area. I stayed here 20 years ago and I find everything about this inn to be as charming today as it was then. *Directions:* From I-95 traveling south, take exit 70, turn right off the ramp to the third building on the left. Traveling north on I-95, turn left off the ramp and right at the second light, go to the end of the road, then turn left to the inn.

BEE AND THISTLE INN
Innkeepers: The Nelson Family
100 Lyme Street
Old Lyme, CT 06371
Tel: (860) 434-1667 or (800) 622-4946
Fax: (860) 434-3402
E-mail: info@beeandthistleinn.com
11 rooms, 1 cottage, Double: $79–$210*,
  *Breakfast not included
Open all year
Credit cards: all major
Restaurant: all meals
Handicap room: none

Ridgefield is one of those glorious country towns in the northwestern corner of Connecticut and the West Lane Inn is perfectly situated for explorations of the area. The inn is set graciously in an elegant 19th-century estate, surrounded by an expanse of lawn, garden, and blooming shrubbery. There's a grand porch spanning the front of the building—a great place to sit and read with a cup of tea. The air-conditioned guestrooms all have queen four-poster beds, private baths, and every amenity a guest might want. All rooms have cable TV, modem access, 24-hour telephone service, and voice mail, and some have fireplaces. Flowered wallpapers are used extensively, adding to the rooms' charm and comfort. Dining is available at the inn next door. There's much to do in this area: great antiquing, good museums and shopping, cross-country skiing, golf, tennis, hiking, ice-skating, and any other sport you'd like to try. The inn has three rooms with kitchens for extended stays—and who wouldn't want to linger in this inn and this area! *Directions:* From New York City take the West Side Highway to Saw Mill River Parkway to exit 6 and turn right on Route 35 east for 12 miles to the inn.

WEST LANE INN
Innkeepers: Maureen Mayer & Deborah Prieger
22 West Lane (Rte. 35)
Ridgefield, CT 06877
Tel: (203) 438-7323
Fax: (203) 438-7325
E-mail: westlanein@aol.com
17 rooms, 3 with kitchens
Double: $125–$185
Open all year
Credit cards: all major
Restaurant: none
Handicap room: none

On a back road north of the town of Salisbury in the northwestern corner of Connecticut, there's a country inn with views to the mountains where you can drink British ale and single-malt whisky, choose from a menu featuring steak and kidney pie, roast goose, and trifle, and enjoy a really good cup of tea. There are several living rooms where you can find a corner for a good conversation or a good book. In addition to the dining room, which is for guests only, the inn also features a pub with a long bar, hand-hewn beams, and dark paneling. The inn's seven bedrooms, all with private bathrooms, are comfortably furnished. One has flowered wallpaper with matching fabric on the king-size canopy bed and an especially comfortable seating area with a good standing lamp for reading. The Tanglewood Music Festival is held nearby and there are hundreds of antique shops in the area. In winter you can enjoy a horse-drawn sleigh ride, go skiing and enjoy country living at its best. The owners are happy to provide a picnic supper for Tanglewood. Also offered are Dickens weekends and special two- and three-night packages. *Directions*: From the Massachusetts Turnpike (I-90) take exit 2 to Route 102 west to Route 7 south to Route 23 west in Great Barrington. At the intersection of Route 41, turn south for 9 miles to the inn on the right.

UNDER MOUNTAIN INN
Innkeepers: Marged & Peter Higginson
482 Undermountain Road (Rte. 41)
Salisbury, CT 06068
Tel: (860) 435-0242
Fax: (860) 435-2379
7 rooms, Double: $175–225*,
  *Includes breakfast, tea & dinner
Open all year
Credit cards: MC, VS
Restaurant for guests only
Handicap room: none

Every once in a while a really wonderful inn is created from an historic structure by a group of very talented artists. Such is The Inn at National Hall where all imaginable comforts are augmented by a staff and level of service both always present yet unobtrusive. Every conceivable amenity is available and there are extra-special touches such as slippers at turn-down time, little readings to take to bed, the next day's weather forecast, and suggestions of things to. This is a great, fabulously decorated inn and you are tempted to cancel all plans just for the privilege of staying within its walls—and that is exactly what I did. I stayed in a corner suite with mustard-painted walls, expansive river views, a king bed with a paisley corolla canopy, and a desk. Painted on the bathroom wall were whimsical *trompe l'oeil* monkeys, which reflected in the mirrors. This inn has polish, charm, and wonderful furnishings, and it uses whimsy in its decor to create an enduring memory of a time spent in total comfort. On the premises there's a fine restaurant, which also provides room service. Westport, just an hour from New York, is a very sophisticated community and no inn could complement the town better than The Inn at National Hall. *Directions*: From New York take the I-95 to exit 17 and turn left to Route 33 for 1½ miles, then after the traffic lights turn immediately right to the inn. From Merritt Parkway leave at exit 41, drive south toward Westport, and in about 2 miles you find the inn on the left.

THE INN AT NATIONAL HALL
Innkeepers: Gene Gorab & Jim Cooper
Two Boston Post Road
Westport, CT 06880
Tel: (203) 221-1351 or (800) 628-4255
Fax: (203) 221-0276
E-mail: info@innatnationalhall.com
15 rooms, Double: $225–$660
Open all year, Credit cards: all major
Restaurant: dinner Tuesday through Saturday
Handicap room: none
www.karenbrown.com/ne/innatnationalhall.html

Maine
Places to Stay-Map 2

Greenville

15

Abbot Village

16

16

95

Rangeley

15

95

Bangor

1A

Hancock Point

15

3

1

Blue Hill

Bar Harbor

Lincolnville

15

Camden

Northeast
Harbor

Waterford

Deer Isle

37

Sunset

9

302

Durham

Wiscasset

Rockland

495

95

302

125

Newcastle

1

Portland

95

1

9

Kennebunkport

Ogunquit

York

● Places to Stay

○ Points of Reference

a	b
c	d

Quadrants

85

The Acadia National Park in Bar Harbor, Maine is one of the most beautiful national parks in America and everyone should try at some time to spend several days soaking up its beauty. Fortunately, a wonderful inn, The Inn at Canoe Point, sits next to the park and as I approached down the driveway, which winds among trees along the edge of the bay, I fell in love with the inn before I even reached it. You enter into the front parlor with its welcoming fireplace and adjoining seating area. From the large hallway stairs climb to the second- and third-floor bedrooms, most of which have mesmerizing views to the bay. The Master Suite has a seating area in front of a gas fireplace, a cherry four-poster queen bed, tiled bathroom, and French doors to a shared deck. The Garden Room also has a queen bed, private entrance, and views of the gardens as well as the bay. The breakfast room on the ground floor has a fireplace and comfortable seating in addition to two tables, each for four people. Floor-to-ceiling windows surrounding two sides of this room give sensational bay views. Equally enticing to my photographer's eye were the views from a series of four high windows that look out into the woods and rocks. *Directions:* From Ellsworth, take Route 3 east about 15 miles to Bar Harbor, through Hulls Cove. A quarter of a mile past the Acadia National Park entrance you see the Canoe Point sign on the left—follow the drive to the ocean and the inn.

THE INN AT CANOE POINT
Innkeepers: Nancy & Tom Cervelli
Eden Street, Route 3, P.O. Box 216
Bar Harbor, ME 04609
Tel: (207) 288-9511, Fax: (207) 288-2870
E-mail: canoe.point@juno.com
3 rooms, 2 suites, Double: $170–$285
Open all year
Credit cards: all major
Restaurant: none
Handicap room: none
www.karenbrown.com/ne/theinnatcanoepoint.html

Nestled in the shade of the pretty trees that line historic West Street, the Manor House Inn is an attractive, soft-yellow, three-story home with shuttered windows, steep pitches and angles to its roof, and lovely wide verandas. Built in 1887 as a lavish 22-room residence, Manor House has now been authentically restored to its original splendor, offering 17 guest accommodations and is listed on the National Register of Historic Places. We had heard from many of our readers about this lovely inn and so were disappointed to learn that it would be closed at the time of our visit. However, I got permission to tour the grounds and peek through windows and could see into the common room on the first floor with its grand piano and ornate Victorian furnishings. Guestrooms, all with private bathrooms, are found in the original Manor House, the two Garden Cottages, or the original Chauffeur's Cottage. The Carriage House is being renovated to provide an additional three luxury rooms. Breakfast begins with freshly baked blueberry muffins and breads, fresh fruit, and cereals, followed by a hot dish such as ham and cheese baked omelet or baked blueberry-stuffed French toast. Manor House's in-town location is only moments from the water and just a few more moments away from all of Bar Harbor's restaurants and galleries. Access to Acadia National Park with its many attractions is less than an hour away. *Directions:* Take Route 3 south and just as you enter Bar Harbor turn left onto West Street (the first cross street). Manor House is three blocks down on the right.

MANOR HOUSE INN
Innkeepers: Mac Noyes & Jim Dennison
106 West Street
Bar Harbor, ME 04609
Tel: (207) 288-3759 or (800) 437-0088
Fax: (207) 288-2974
E-mail: manor@acadia.net
8 rooms, 7 suites, 2 cottages, Double: $95–$225
Open May to mid-November, Credit cards: all major
Restaurant: none, Handicap room: none
www.karenbrown.com/ne/manorhouseinn.html

The Ullikana, built in 1885, is one of the few remaining original cottages in Bar Harbor. Though located within an easy walk of all the town's activities—restaurants, galleries, and shops are at hand for you to enjoy—it provides a quiet haven overlooking the water. The 16 rooms, all with king or queen beds, are situated in one of two adjoining buildings painted a sunny yellow, which makes them seem so bright and cheery. When I toured the inn it was closed for the winter and the owners were taking the opportunity to paint and remodel in advance of the coming high season. The guestrooms I viewed were large and airy and painted in colors appropriate to an oceanside town in summer. Some of the inn's rooms have views of the water and the boating activity for which Bar Harbor is so well known. The common rooms are of a dark wood—appropriate to the era in which the inn was built—and the furnishings of the period are an integral part of the inn's mood and setting. Breakfasts are served either in the dining room or in the garden, which during the summer months in this delightful community would definitely be the place to be. If you like the Tudor style of architecture as much as I do, I think that you will find the Ullikana a fun place to spend a night or two. *Directions*: Take Route 3 to Bar Harbor, turn left onto Cottage Street, right on Main Street, then left after the Trust Company building. Follow the gravel road towards the water.

ULLIKANA
Innkeepers: Helene Harton & Roy Kasindorf
16 The Field
Bar Harbor, ME 04609
Tel: (207) 288-9552, Fax: (207) 288-3682
16 rooms, Double: $135–$250
Open May through October
Credit cards: all major
Restaurant: none
Handicap room: none

What I love about The Blue Hill Inn (c.1830) is that it's right in the heart of a picture-perfect, historic little town, which has a history that stretches back to when the town was first settled in 1777. The Blue Hill Inn is exceptionally comfortable, with friendly and helpful innkeepers: Mary and Don will help you find that out-of-the-way antique shop or point you in the direction of a good restaurant or a leisurely drive. There are eleven bedrooms and one luxury suite. Rooms at the front are on the main street, so they get some traffic noise but this is an early-to-bed town, so a good night's sleep should not be a problem. I stayed in one of the front bedrooms and it just plain felt comfortable, with a queen bed, a chair or two for reading, and a private bath. Each evening the inn serves wine and hors d'oeuvres and by prior arrangement a candlelight dinner may be planned for your special occasion. Breakfast offers a choice of five entrees. *Directions*: Take the Maine Turnpike to Augusta, then Route 3 east to Belfast, continuing east through Bucksport. Take Route 15 south to Blue Hill. Bear right at the Blue Hill Inn sign on Route 177 east (4½ miles to the inn).

THE BLUE HILL INN
Innkeepers: Mary & Don Hartley
Union St, P.O. Box 403
Blue Hill, ME 04614
Tel: (207) 374-2844 or (800) 826-7415
Fax: (207) 374-2829
E-mail: bluehillinn@hotmail.com
10 rooms, 1 suite, 1 cottage
Double: $145–$260
Closed December to mid-May
Credit cards: all major
Restaurant: special dinners by arrangement
Handicap room
www.karenbrown.com/ne/thebluehillinn.html

In one of the prettiest villages on the Maine coast, set high above the harbor, is Camden Windward House. There are eight bedrooms, several with their own private entrances, all air-conditioned and comfortably decorated with flowered wallpapers and Victorian-era furnishings. Many of the rooms have sitting areas or at least chairs where you can read and relax and all have TV and telephones with data ports. Allergy-free feather beds guarantee a great night's sleep and that's exactly what I had when I stayed in one of the rooms with its own separate entrance: mine was on the second floor and had a separate sitting room with TV. From its window I could look down and out to the harbor with its fishing boats and sailing vessels. There's nothing like the fresh sea air to work up an appetite for a dinner featuring freshly caught seafood and your hosts are happy to help you select a restaurant and make a reservation for you. Breakfast usually includes a choice of eight hot entrees, ranging from eggs to pancakes. Camden is the host harbor for many seafaring schooners on which you can take a week's cruise along the coast, either helping with the sailing or relaxing and soaking up the sun on deck. *Directions:* From Boston take I-95 north to Route 295 to exit 22 in Brunswick to Route 1 to Camden. The inn is one block north of town on the left.

CAMDEN WINDWARD HOUSE
Innkeepers: Charlotte & Del Lawrence
Six High Street
Camden, ME 04843
Tel: (207) 236-9656, Fax: (207) 230-0433
E-mail: bnb@windwardhouse.com
8 rooms, Double: $160–$230
Open all year
Credit cards: all major
Restaurant: none
Handicap room: none
www.karenbrown.com/ne/camdenwindwardhouse.html

Just 4 miles north of Camden in the little village of Lincolnville Beach there's an inn sitting at the water's edge that provides an idyllic place for you to rest and listen to the water lapping at the shore and the wind sighing in the pines. The Inn at Sunrise Point, consisting of the main house and four cottages named after Maine's most famous artists, offers comfortably decorated guestrooms of great charm, each containing a wood-burning fireplace. Bedrooms have either queen or king beds, individually controlled thermostats, telephones, TV/VCRs, and bathrooms with large tubs and plush robes. In the cottages there are two-person spa tubs, wet bars, and private decks. A full breakfast is served either in the glass conservatory of the main house or in the privacy of your own room. This inn is nicely located for exploring all of the wonders of the Camden region and at the end of a day of excursions you can return to the inn to enjoy evening hors d'oeuvres sitting by the fire in the cherry-paneled library. I can imagine nothing nicer than to rest in this setting for days on end, venturing out to the shops and the restaurants and yet taking full advantage of the spectacular setting at the water's edge. It's the sounds or maybe the absence of them that make this inn and its location so wonderful. *Directions:* Take exit 22 from I-95 in Brunswick, following Route 1 north to Camden. Continue through Camden and 4 miles farther on turn right at fire road #9 and drive down to the inn.

THE INN AT SUNRISE POINT
Innkeepers: Jackie & Richard Diehl
P.O. Box 1344, Lincolnville Beach
Camden, ME 04843
Tel: (207) 236-7716 or (800) 435-6278
Fax: (207) 236-0820
E-mail: info@sunrisepoint.com
3 rooms, 4 cottages
Double: $175–$225, Cottage: $250–$375
Open May to November
Credit cards: all major, Restaurant: none
Handicap room: none
www.karenbrown.com/ne/innatsunrisepoint.html

When was the last time you heard the sound of a bosun's pipe announcing that breakfast was ready and you were serenaded by the innkeepers at your morning repast? These are some of the fun touches you'll enjoy when you stay at the Maine Stay in Camden. Camden is one of those picturesque towns surrounded by hills from which you peer down into a harbor of schooners and boating activity—for me as mesmerizing as staring into a wood-burning fireplace. The Maine Stay is delightfully decorated and shipshape in every respect, and you'll find any one of the rooms to be totally comfortable for as long as you can stay. There's a variety of accommodation both in the main house and the attached carriage house, from the two-bedroom Stitchery Suite with its own sitting room to the cozy, old-fashioned Smith Room hung with old portraits. There are two parlors with Oriental rugs and period furnishings, a third-floor sitting room with TV and VCR, and, of course, a porch. A huge Aga stove warms the kitchen and bakes all the wonderful food that you'll enjoy at breakfast. You can walk to everything in town and the innkeepers are happy to steer you in the right direction for all the interesting places to visit in the area. *Directions:* Take I-95 to Route 1 to Camden. The inn is three blocks north of the village.

MAINE STAY
Innkeepers: Donny & Peter Smith, Diana Robson
22 High Street
Camden, ME 04843
Tel: (207) 236-9636
Fax: (207) 236-0621
E-mail: innkeeper@mainestay.com
8 rooms, Double: $100–$150
Open all year
Credit cards: all major
Restaurant: none
Handicap room: none

Pilgrim's Inn, an historic 1793 Colonial, overlooks Northwest Harbor and a picturesque millpond on Deer Isle in Penobscot Bay. The setting is magnificent and while I visited in the winter, I can easily imagine how enchanting the gardens would be in the spring through fall and how peaceful it would be sitting in the backyard overlooking the beautiful waterfront scenery. The decor is warm and inviting and furnishings respect the history and character of the island. The inn has pine floors, several large fireplaces, and antique furnishings, with warm Colonial colors enhancing the cozy feeling of comfort. Thirteen lovely guestrooms are found in the main house but if you are traveling with children, you might want to opt for one of the two self-catering apartments found in a separate building. Gourmet dinners featuring creative American cuisine are served in the barn dining room with its hand-hewn beams and vaulted ceiling. While I would be tempted to stay put and enjoy Deer Isle and neighboring coastal villages, the inn is a good base for visiting Acadia National Park, an hour away, and Isle au Haut (40 minutes by ferry). At the inn's doorstep you can hike, bike, and go boating, while nearby are tennis, golf, and several good art galleries. *Directions:* From Boston take I-95 north to Augusta and Route 3 to Belfast, then follow Route 1 north to Route 15. Turn right onto Route 15 (south), heading for Deer Isle through the Blue Hill Peninsula. In the village turn right onto Main Street (the 15A)—the inn is one block down on the left.

PILGRIM'S INN
Innkeepers: Jean & Dud Hendrick
P.O. Box 69
Deer Isle, ME 04627
Tel: (207) 348-6615, Fax: (207) 348-7769
E-mail: dudhe@ctel.net
13 rooms, 2 apartments, Double: $160–$225*,
  *Includes dinner
Open mid-May to mid-October
Credit cards: all major
Restaurant: breakfast & dinner
Handicap room: none

The Bagley House Inn is just ten minutes from downtown Freeport, situated on 6 acres of countryside dotted with fields and woods. Nearby in Freeport is the internationally renowned L. L. Bean store—open 24 hours a day. Freeport is also home to many discount stores so you can shop here well beyond the point of dropping from exhaustion. The Bagley House, a wonderful 18th-century home turned into an inn, provides a quiet refuge from all this hustle and bustle. Its eight guestrooms, located in the main house and the recently built carriage house, just a few steps from the main house, are attractively and simply decorated with antiques or beautifully hand-crafted pieces and hand-sewn quilts on the beds. Each room has its own private bath. One room has a double bed plus a ¾ bed for a third person and the inn will provide porta-cribs for children. The rooms in the carriage house are somewhat larger than in the main house but you'll give up the wide pine floors and the charm of staying in a building from the 18th century. Full breakfasts are served at the 8-foot antique baker's table in the magnificent country kitchen with its hand-hewn beams, vaulted ceiling with loft, and large fireplace with beehive oven. There are two parlors to relax in, each with a large welcoming fireplace. *Directions*: Take I-95 to Freeport, exit 20. Turn right as you get off onto Route 136, then right to the inn after approximately 6 miles.

THE BAGLEY HOUSE INN
Innkeepers: Susan Backhouse & Suzanne O'Connor
1290 Royalsborough Road
Durham, ME 04222
Tel: (207) 865-6566 or (800) 765-1772
Fax: (207) 355-5878
E-mail: bglyhse@aol.com
8 rooms, Double: $110–$150
Open all year
Credit cards: all major
Restaurant: none
Handicap room
www.karenbrown.com/ne/bagleyhouseinn.html

Magic is everywhere up in this northern part of Maine—particularly at The Lodge at Moosehead Lake. Roger, one of the owners and creators of this paradise, is the consummate innkeeper: it would be hard to imagine someone more devoted to seeing that his guests experience all that this part of Maine can offer. Here you can sit on a porch and overlook the broad waters and islands of the largest lake in Maine; go dogsledding, snowshoeing, snowmobiling, and cross-country and downhill skiing in the winter; enjoy mountain biking, white-water rafting, touring by plane, hiking, canoeing, or fly-fishing in some secret stream or lake. And where else can you go on a moose safari? The other half of this team is Jennifer, the visionary and creator of all the inn's decor. The five bedrooms and three suites are nothing short of fabulous. I stayed in the Bear Room in a hand-carved four-poster queen bed with bears carved into and perched on its posts. There was a hand-carved bear bench at the foot of the bed, two different sitting areas, and a gas corner fireplace with a chair nearby for gazing out at the lake. Twigs are used to create borders instead of moldings and to simulate picture hangings. *Directions:* Take I-95 to Newport, Route 7 north to Dexter, then Route 23 north to Guilford, where you take Route 15 north to Greenville. (1½ hours by car from Bangor, 2½ hours from Portland, 4½ hours from Boston.)

THE LODGE AT MOOSEHEAD LAKE
Innkeepers: Jennifer & Roger Cauchi
Upon Lily Bay Road
Greenville, ME 04441
Tel: (207) 695-4400, Fax (207) 695-2281
E-mail: innkeeper@lodgeatmooseheadlake.com
5 rooms, 3 suites, Double $175–$325, Suite: $250–$425
Open December 30 to March 19, May 1 to October 25
Credit cards: MC, VS
Restaurant: dinner Mondays & Thursdays in season,
  Saturday night off season
Handicap room: none
www.karenbrown.com/ne/thelodgeatmooseheadlake.html

The Crocker House Country Inn is a lovely three-story, gray-shingle home, trimmed in white, dating back to 1884. The setting on Hancock Point is very picturesque and quiet, and if you arrive by boat, it's just a short stroll over the hill from the harbor, Frenchman Bay. The current owners, the Malabys, have restored the property and created a warm and inviting ambiance both in the decor and welcoming service. Each of the guestrooms is individually decorated, although all have a country flavor and beds are topped with wonderful old quilts. Two bedrooms are located in the former carriage house, which also provides an additional common room and a spa. Guests have a lovely living room and two sitting rooms, one of which boasts a piano and live music on weekends. The inn is probably best known for its food, which you can enjoy in two dining rooms. The restaurant, open to both resident and non-resident guests, offers breakfast, dinner, and Sunday brunch from July through Labor Day. Always busy and quite popular, the inn hosts many weddings, family reunions, and small business retreats. Attractions include a croquet court, clay tennis courts, antiquing, golf, kayaking, and biking, and the fabulous Acadia National Park about 20 minutes away. *Directions*: From Ellsworth travel 8 miles east on Route 1, turn right on Point Road and go 5 miles to the inn (on the right).

CROCKER HOUSE COUNTRY INN
Innkeepers: Elizabeth & Richard Malaby
HC 77, Box 171
Hancock Point, ME 04640
Tel: (207) 422-6806, Fax: (207) 422-3105
E-mail: crocker@acadia.net
11 rooms, Double: $90–$145
Open April to New Year's Day
Credit cards: all major
Restaurant: breakfast, dinner & Sunday brunch,
  July 1 through Labor Day
Handicap room

Just outside the village of Kennebunkport yet within an easy walk of the shops, galleries, and restaurants is Bufflehead Cove, an inn set at the edge of a saltwater inlet. The inn, formerly a private home, now has five guestrooms, a cozy living room, and a dining room. The Balcony Room has water views, a private balcony, gas fireplace, king bed, and whirlpool tub. The queen-bedded River Room, with its collections of folk art and its ceiling shimmering with sunlight reflected off the water, has a private balcony where you can sit and read or enjoy a glass of wine. A delicious full breakfast is served either in the dining room, on the porch by the water, or on the open sunny deck. One breakfast menu included freshly squeezed orange juice, ginger-poached pears in an English custard sauce, apple-stuffed French toast, maple-glazed sausage, and either coffee or a selection of teas. The inn serves wine and cheese in the evening and the innkeepers will be glad to review restaurant options for dinner and then make reservations for you. The personable dog, Lili, adds to the enjoyment of your stay. *Directions:* Leave the Maine Turnpike I-95 at exit 3 onto Route 35 south. At the intersection of Routes 1 and 35 continue on Route 35 for 3-1/10 miles to the inn sign on the left. Follow the lane down to the water.

BUFFLEHEAD COVE
Innkeepers: Harriet & James Gott
P.O. Box 499
Kennebunkport, ME 04046
Tel & fax: (207) 967-3879
E-mail: info@buffleheadcove.com
5 rooms, Double: $165–$350, 1 Cottage: $525
Open all year
Credit cards: all major
Restaurant: none
Handicap room: none
www.karenbrown.com/ne/buffleheadcove.html

The town green sloping down from the Captain Lord Mansion to the river gives this very stylishly decorated inn a very prominent position that befits its splendid interior. The decor is lavish, from the lovely wallpapers that adorn the walls in the halls to those in the bedrooms, each of which is named after a ship built here in an earlier era. Paintings in ornate frames hang everywhere—an obvious love of the owners who have searched long and hard to find the touches that make this inn so special. I stayed in the Cactus room with a king four-poster bed, gas fireplace, and a bath with double vanity and shower. Other bedrooms have canopy beds and whirlpool tubs for two. A delicious complete breakfast with a hot entree is served in the kitchen most mornings at two long tables where you have a good opportunity to meet and talk to your fellow guests. The parlor has a large fireplace that was burning warmly on the occasion of my visit and comfortable chairs in which to sit, relax, and have a good conversation or a cup of afternoon tea. Captain Lord Mansion is a quiet haven just a few minutes' walk from the heart of Kennebunkport with its many shops, activities, and restaurants. *Directions:* Take the I-95 (Maine Turnpike) to exit 3, go left on Route 35 for 5½ miles then east on Route 9. Turn left over the bridge and first right in the square, to Ocean Ave. Go 3/10 mile and turn left into Green Street.

CAPTAIN LORD MANSION
Innkeepers: Bev Davis & Rick Litchfield
P.O. Box 800
Kennebunkport, ME 04046
Tel: (207) 967-3141, Fax: (207) 967-3172
E-mail: captain@biddeford.com
15 rooms, 1 suite, Double: $199–$399
Open all year
Credit cards: all major
Restaurant: none
Handicap room: none
www.karenbrown.com/ne/captainlordmansion.html

As I walked through the doorway of my bedroom, I saw reflected in the antique dressing-table mirror the bed with its attractive floral bedspread and knew that my stay would be a comfortable one. The exterior of this beautiful 1860 Victorian with wrap-around porches and an impressive cupola sets the tone for the style that you expect inside, where a magnificent suspended spiral staircase winds its way up from the entrance hall. Guestrooms are divided between the main house and cottages on the grounds and there are many variations of amenities so be sure to discuss your preference for a fireplace, whirlpool-tub, sitting room, kitchen, or microwave when you make your reservation. If you are staying in one of the cottages, you have the option of either coming to the inn for a full breakfast or having a breakfast basket delivered to your door. The Maine Stay is located within a very short walk of Dock Square, the center of all the activity in this little seaside village. Antiques, clothing, and remembrances of your visit are all available in the many fine shops. There are several good restaurants that specialize in freshly caught local seafood. *Directions:* Take exit 3 from the Maine Turnpike (I-95), turning left on Route 35 south. Go 5½ miles to Route 9, turn left, then go over the bridge and through the village to the stop sign. Turn right on Maine Street: the inn is three blocks down.

THE MAINE STAY INN & COTTAGES
Innkeepers: Carol & Lindsay Copeland
34 Maine Street, P.O. Box 500A
Kennebunkport, ME 04046
Tel: (207) 967-2117 or (800) 950-2117
Fax: (207) 967-8757
E-mail: innkeeper@mainestayinn.com
4 rooms, 4 suites, 9 cottages
Double: $105–$195, Suite: $135–$250,
* Cottage: $95–$250*
Open all year (weekends only January to March)
Credit cards: all major
Restaurant: none
Handicap room: none

Although the Old Fort Inn only has 16 rooms, it's a mini-resort with its own swimming pool, tennis court, horseshoes, and shuffleboard. Air-conditioned guestrooms, in either the circa-1880 converted barn or the carriage house, are stylishly decorated with antiques and attractive furnishings and each is equipped with a wet bar with a small refrigerator, TV, and telephone. I visited one room done in black and shades of gray and beige and found it to be very attractive. The fishnet canopy bed was covered by a bedspread that echoed the room's attractive color scheme. There was a separate living room with comfortable chairs and a view out to the inn's pool and gardens. For decades I have shopped at the inn's well-stocked antique store in the main building. The inn, set in its own private compound of 7 acres, is only a block from the ocean and 1¼ miles from the shops, galleries, and restaurants of Kennebunkport. Its residential neighborhood at the end of the road gives you peace and quiet and a real sense of being away from all the hustle and bustle of the busier section of this popular tourist town. The inn prepares a full gourmet breakfast, which you can eat on the porch overlooking the swimming pool or beside the pool on a nice morning. *Directions:* Take exit 3 from the Maine Turnpike (I-95) then turn left on Route 35 for 5½ miles. Turn left at the light onto Route 9 for 3/10 mile then right onto Ocean Ave for 9/10 mile to the Colony Hotel where you take a left. Turn right at the T-junction and follow signs for 3/10 mile to the inn.

OLD FORT INN
Innkeepers: Sheila & David Aldrich
8 Old Fort Ave, P.O. Box M
Kennebunkport, ME 04046
Tel: (207) 967-5353, Fax: (207) 967-4547
E-mail: ofi@ispchannel.com
16 rooms, Double: $150–$350
Open mid-April to mid-December
Credit cards: all major
Restaurant: none
Handicap room: none
www.karenbrown.com/ne/oldfortinn.html

Just beyond the hustle and bustle of the historic town of Kennebunkport sits the White Barn Inn, an inn whose restaurant is of such renown that you may tend to forget that it also has wonderful accommodations. Eighteen guestrooms and seven suites are found in the main building, the pool house, and the carriage house. All the rooms have been meticulously restored and furnished with period furnishings, with a great eye for detail. Amenities include TVs, CD radios, fresh flowers, bathrooms with whirlpool tubs, thick robes, and elegant toiletries—and I loved the wood-burning fireplaces. My room had softly painted walls and two comfortable upholstered chairs with an ottoman on which to rest my feet after a long day of walking around Kennebunkport. The restaurant is one of only five AAA five-diamond restaurants in New England and the special focus on locally caught seafood makes the ever-changing menu a real treat. Complimentary bicycles are available for cycling the short distance to the village or for riding down to the ocean beach for a walk or a swim. If you prefer swimming in warmer water, try the inn's heated swimming pool. Golf, tennis, horseback riding, deep-sea fishing, whale watching, and sailing are all available close by. The nearby wildlife preserve is a great place to walk and to enjoy the special beauty of Maine's rugged coast. *Directions*: Leave the Maine Turnpike (I-95) at exit 3 for Kennebunk, then take Route 35 south for 7 miles to Kennebunkport. Cross the light at Route 9 and the inn is on the right after ¼ mile.

WHITE BARN INN
Director: Maureen Violette
Beach Avenue, P.O. Box 560 C
Kennebunkport, ME 04046
Tel: (207) 967-2321, Fax: (207) 967-1100
E-mail: innkeeper@whitebarninn.com
16 rooms, 8 suites, 1 cottage
Double: $230–$395, Suite: $395–$595
Open all year
Credit cards: all major
Restaurant: dinner
Handicap room

The Newcastle Inn, looking down sloping lawns with lovely gardens to the water's edge, commands an enviable position in the charming seacoast village of Newcastle with its many cute shops and wonderful bookstore. The inn is as lovely inside as out and has recently received a fresh look with new wallpapers, carpeting, and reupholstered furniture. A very special touch is the living-room floor, which has been hand-painted in the most charming of designs. Off the living room, an enclosed porch with beautiful views from its many windows is a great place to sit in the afternoon with a book and a glass of wine. The restaurant menu changes daily and specializes in the best of the local foods—especially seafood. The breakfast I had when I stayed there was wonderful, with an omelet preceded by fresh fruit and juice. I stayed in a room on the third floor looking out to the water. While simply furnished, it was very comfortable with its floral wallpaper and upholstered chair where I enjoyed reading in the evening. The rooms do not have individual telephones but off the living room there is an anteroom with a desk where you can make a private telephone call. *Directions:* From Coastal Route 1 travel 6 miles north of Wiscasset Bridge. Turn right on River Road and the inn is on your right after half a mile.

THE NEWCASTLE INN
Innkeepers: Rebeccca & Howard Levitan
60 River Road
Newcastle, ME 04553
Tel: (207) 563-5685 or (800) 832-8669
Fax: (207) 563-6877
E-mail: innkeep@newcastleinn.com
12 rooms, 2 suites, Double: $145–$250
Closed January
Credit cards: all major
Restaurant: breakfast, dinner by reservation
 in season except Monday, weekends only in winter
Handicap room: none

The more northerly section of the Maine coast consists of fingers of land that run down to the ocean, creating long inlets and miles of coastline settled with centuries-old little fishing villages. Here you find Northeast Harbor, a very popular, upscale community of summer homes. The Grey Rock Inn, formerly a private mansion, is situated on 7 acres overlooking the harbor, the lighthouse, and the outer islands off Mount Desert. Its seven rooms and one suite are elegantly decorated. The Sun guestroom has twelve double-hung windows and a set of French doors wrapping the room. Through the doors is a private porch and veranda with eight granite pillars. The room comfortably contains a king and single beds, a secretary, sofa, three stained-glass lamps, a pair of window seats, and a brick wood-burning fireplace. The Butterfly room is lovely, with views up and down the length of Northeast Harbor, pretty silvery wallpaper that comes alive with hundreds of butterflies, a handsome white wrought-iron-and-brass antique double bed, white wicker chairs, and a painted bureau. The inn provides a full breakfast and there are many restaurants nearby for dinner. The area offers many sporting activities, whale watching, shops, and galleries, and Acadia National Park is a just short drive away. *Directions*: From Ellsworth follow Route 3/198 on Mount Desert Island. Just before Northeast Harbor the inn is on the right bordering the Acadia National Park.

GREY ROCK INN
Innkeepers: Janet, Karl & Adam Millett
Harbourside Road
Northeast Harbor, ME 04662
Tel: (207) 276-9360 (summer), (207) 244-4437 (winter)
Fax: (207) 276-9894
7 rooms, 1 suite, Double: $155–$375
Open mid-May through October
Credit cards: all major
Restaurant: none, Handicap room: none
www.karenbrown.com/ne/greyrockinn.html

Hartwell House is located just outside Perkins Cove, one of those scenic Maine lobster-fishing villages. There are many inns in the region and yet Hartwell House, a lovely, traditional New England home, is always described as the most elegant and very beautiful. The inn consists of two buildings that face each other across a street going down to the harbor. Set on an acre and a half of lush green lawn and gardens, the elegant main building houses the common rooms: the sun porch, the dining room, and a lovely sitting room. Attached to the main house, which also houses eight guestrooms, are two studio bedrooms that step up to their own outside entrance. Across the street all the bedrooms have a terrace or balcony and there are three suites. The inn serves a full gourmet breakfast and afternoon tea. A short walk from the inn is the Marginal Way footpath, one of the most picturesque spots on the coast of lower Maine. There is much to do here—beaches to enjoy, fishing, golf, tennis, sailing, galleries to visit, antiquing, and summer theatre. *Directions:* Take exit 4 from the Maine Turnpike north, turning left on Route 1 (north) for 4-4/10 miles. Turn right on Pine Hill, left on Shore, and go 2/10 mile to the inn on the left. From the Maine Turnpike south, take exit 2, go left on Route 109, right on Route 1 for 6 miles, then left on Shore Road for 6/10 mile to the inn on the right.

HARTWELL HOUSE
Innkeepers: Trisha & James Hartwell,
  Tracey & Christopher Anderson
118 Shore Road
Ogunquit, ME 03907
Tel: (207) 646-7210 or (800) 235-8883
Fax: (207) 646-6032
E-mail: hartwell@cybertours.com
11 rooms, 2 studios, 3 suites
Double & Studio: $90–$170, Suite: $145–$190
Open all year, Credit cards: all major
Restaurant: all meals in season,
  Weekends only in the spring & fall
Handicap room: none

A small city like Portland needs to have a great inn so that you can settle in to explore all that there is to do here for a day or two or three. The Pomegranate Inn is just the place, located in the historic district and within an easy walk of all the sights. Its totally conforming external historical appearance belies the eclectic decorating that you'll find inside. The artwork—pictures and sculpture—demands your attention and your involvement. Whether you understand it or not doesn't matter—but you will love it just the same. The inn's eight rooms, one suite, and a garden room are all beautifully decorated with antiques and show more of that eclectic touch with walls sporting hand-painted flowers. It would be hard to beat the carriage house for real seclusion or the guestroom that has its own private terrace. Every room has a private bath, telephone, and television and some have fireplaces. This inn provides a different visual experience in a traditional setting and I think you'll like it as much as I did. There's wine to greet your arrival and a full breakfast is served at a long table in the dining room. *Directions:* From northbound I-95 take I-295, leaving at exit 4 for Route 1A. Turn immediately left onto Danforth Street, first left onto Vaughan, then right on Carroll for 1 block. From the north, take I-295 to exit 6A to Route 77, which is also State Street, turn right on Pine, then left on Neal.

POMEGRANATE INN
Innkeeper: Isabel Smiles
49 Neal Street
Portland, ME 04102
Tel: (207) 772-1006 or (800) 356-0408
Fax: (207) 773-4426
8 rooms, 1 suite, 1 garden room
Double: $95–$205
Open all year
Credit cards: all major
Restaurant: none
Handicap room

Overlooking the majestic beauty of Penobscot Bay at the end of a long dirt road on one of the fingers of land jutting out to sea is The Goose Cove Lodge. With its 23 cabins, rooms, and suites, this inn provides a rustic yet sophisticated setting for a wonderful stay on the Maine coast. The cabins are scattered about the grounds, some rather near one another and others tucked back in the woods where you have total privacy. All are rustic in character and furnishings, most having fireplaces and some having sundecks. This is a great place to bring children, with lots of activities organized for them and their own separate dinnertime. In season the cabins are available only on a weekly basis. The drive to this inn takes a bit of time and it's my guess that once you arrive and settle in you'll be perfectly delighted not to move because right on site you'll find sailing, kayaking, hiking, biking, tennis, and nature trails. The lodge has a great restaurant with a fine menu featuring fresh local ingredients. Three meals a day are served during the May to October season but there are four cottages available year round where you can stay with either breakfast or breakfast and dinner. This is a special place to go for a relaxing break away from it all. *Directions:* Take Route 1 north through Bucksport, then Route 15 south to Deer Isle Village. Turn right on Main Street, travel 3 miles to Goose Cove Road, and turn right to the lodge.

THE GOOSE COVE LODGE
Innkeepers: Joanne & Dom Parisi
Goose Cove Road, P.O. Box 40
Sunset, ME 04683
Tel: (207) 348-2508 or (800) 728-1963
Fax: (207) 348-2624
E-mail: goosecove@goosecovelodge.com
23 cabins, suites & rooms
Double: $146–$226, $190–$460 with dinner
Open May to October (3 cottages all year)
Credit cards: all major
Restaurant: all meals
Handicap room: none

I first learned of Waterford when my dear friend decided to return to her family ties in Maine, and when I think of Waterford I think of an idyllic, classic New England town with its white steeple church on a grassy knoll. The Waterford Inne, a bed and breakfast with eight bedrooms and one suite, provides a terrific place to stay. The inn is a 19th-century farmhouse on a country lane amidst 25 acres of fields and woods—just viewing it tells you that this is another of those homes that now serves guests as it once did the original family. The guestrooms are uniquely decorated, mixing the warmth of antique furnishings with contemporary comforts in their modern bathrooms. The simple but elegant common rooms echo the decor of the bedrooms, with antiques and art, barnboard, brass, pewter, and primitives. With advance notice the innkeepers will provide dinner but there are also numerous restaurants nearby. Skiing and other winter sports are available in the area and in the summer there are many musical events, while antiquing is fun year round. *Directions:* Leave the Maine Turnpike at exit 11, following Route 26 north for about 28 miles to Norway where you pick up Route 118 west. Drive 9 miles to Route 37, turn left, and travel half a mile to Springer's Store. Turn right and the inn is half a mile up the hill.

THE WATERFORD INNE
Innkeeper: Barbara Vanderzanden
Chadbourne Road, P.O. Box 149
Waterford, ME 04088
Tel & fax: (207) 583-4037
E-mail: inne@gwi.net
8 rooms, 1 suite
Double: $80–$120
Open all year
Credit cards: AX
Restaurant: dinner for guests & public by reservation
Handicap room: none
www.karenbrown.com/ne/thewaterfordinne.html

Sitting at the end of a long country road, The Squire Tarbox Inn, a farmhouse with sections from 1763–1825, listed on the National Register of Historic Places, exudes the peace and quiet of the countryside surrounding it. This rambling Colonial farm is distinguished by its herd of goats, which produce some excellent, award-winning cheese. While you may simply stop to buy the cheese, it would be even better to plan some time to stay here and to enjoy the splendor of being in the country. Sure, you can walk the path that leads to the water's edge and do some boating but I'd settle in with a good book in front of a wood-burning fire and let time slide by. For those who do want to venture out, there's harbors and beaches nearby, plenty of antiquing, shopping at discount stores, or exploring the countryside, as well as several fascinating museums with a variety of different themes. The inn's 11 bedrooms are simply but very comfortably decorated. Dinner is served in the dining room at tables dressed with tablecloths and posies of flowers from the garden. It consists of five courses featuring fresh seasonal ingredients and always includes some of the inn's own goat cheese, prepared in a variety of styles. There is a set menu but dietary needs are taken into account. *Directions:* Take the Maine Turnpike to Route 1, traveling north through Brunswick. Seven miles north of Bath Bridge, turn right on Route 144 for 8½ miles—the inn is on the right.

THE SQUIRE TARBOX INN
Innkeepers: Karen & Bill Mitman
Westport Island, P.O. Box 1181
Wiscasset, ME 04578
Tel: (207) 882-7693, Fax: (207) 882-7107
E-mail: squiretarbox@ime.net
11 rooms, Double: $112–$179, $152–$251 with dinner
Open mid-May to late October
Credit cards: all major
Restaurant: dinner for guests & public by reservation
Handicap room: none

Once you cross into Maine life seems different: first there's the smell of the sea air; then there are views down picturesque inlets of open water and the rise and fall of the ocean tides; then you see the signs for lobster—and you realize that you are in a place where the people, the food and the scenery are unique. At the Dockside Guest Quarters you are immediately captured by the setting on the water and the fishing boats rounding the channel buoys on their way to and from a day's work. There are 19 rooms and 6 suites, simply but comfortably decorated so that you are not distracted from exquisite views across the inlet. The guestrooms are located in several buildings all having the same great location and view. I stayed in one of the suites with a nicely furnished living room, bedroom and a full bath. Your visit will be enhanced by your hosts, the Lustys, who encourage to you take advantage of all the coast-oriented activities such as boating, fishing, beach walking, and biking. Nearby you find whale watching, lobstering, golf, tennis, summer theatre, lighthouses, and outlet stores for the avid shopper. Lunch and dinner are served in the inn's restaurant where you can dine on the porch overlooking the harbor, while breakfast is served in the Maine house. *Directions:* From I-95 heading north, take exit 4, head south on Route 1. Turn left at the first light to Route 1A, go through York Village, then turn right on Route 103 and follow signs to the inn.

DOCKSIDE GUEST QUARTERS
Innkeepers: The Lusty Family
Harris Island Road, P.O. Box 205
York, ME 03909
Tel: (207) 363-2868 or (800) 270-1977
Fax: (207) 363-1977
E-mail: info@docksidegq.com
19 rooms, 6 suites, Double: $80–$140*, Suite: $110–$210*,
  *Breakfast not included
Open all year, weekends only November to May
Restaurant: lunch and dinner, Credit cards: all major
Handicap room
www.karenbrown.com/ne/docksideguestquarters.html

Massachusetts
Places to Stay-Map 3

Williamston

Greenfield

Deerfield

Lenox

kbridge

uth
nont

Rockport

Concord

Marblehead

Cambridge

Boston

Sudbury

Auburn

Sturbridge

Provincetown

Sandwich

Barnstable
Village

Eastham

Orleans

Chatham

Brewster

Yarmouth Port

South Yarmouth

Falmouth

Vineyard
Haven

Nantucket

Wauwinet

Martha's Vineyard

Edgartown

Nantucket Island

● Places to Stay
○ Points of Reference

| a | b | Quadrants |
| c | d | |

Barnstable is one of those wonderfully quaint villages found on the north shore of Cape Cod and Ashley Manor is an inn worthy of a night's visit. Dating back to 1699, the inn sits back from the road in 2 acres of landscaped gardens surrounded by high hedges. Ashley Manor reveals its age with its wide-board flooring, large open-hearth fireplaces, and hand-glazed wainscoting. This inn is both elegant and warm, with beautiful decor and furnishings that include Oriental rugs, antiques, and handsome country furniture. Relax in the comfortable parlor and library or enjoy the privacy of your lovely room which is equipped with everything you need for a pampered stay—fresh flowers, imported chocolates, and the finest soaps, shampoos, and lotions. All but one has a cozy fireplace and the suites offer the additional luxury of large whirlpool tubs. Breakfast is served in the parlor, the formal dining room, or in good weather on the terrace. If you have any spare time, you can play tennis. *Directions:* From Boston take Route 3 south to Sagamore Bridge onto Cape Cod, then follow Route 6 to exit 6. Turn immediately left onto Route 132 north to Route 6A and go about 3 miles through Barnstable Village to the traffic light. The inn is 6/10 mile down on the left.

ASHLEY MANOR
Innkeepers: Mary Ann O'Brien & Donald Bain
3660 Olde Kings Highway, P.O. Box 856
Barnstable, MA 02630
Tel: (508) 362-8044 or (888) 535-2246
Fax: (508) 362-9927
E-mail: ashleymn@capecod.net
2 rooms, 4 suites, Double: $135–$195
Open all year
Credit cards: all major
Restaurant: none
Handicap room: none

This 1643 inn sits high on a hill with views of the village of Barnstable, the harbor, and the ocean. The simple rustic quality of this six-bedroom inn, each of whose rooms have a snug bathroom with whirlpool tub, provides the visitor with an alternative to the more formal and highly decorated inns found elsewhere on the Cape. The inn was built of 12-by 12-inch rough-cut timbers and many of the walls are covered in rough burlap. The innkeepers are charming and determined to make your visit to their inn and to the Cape a special memory. The third-floor suites, my first choice, have comfortable seating in front of a view to the ocean you can hardly tear yourself away from—Cape Cod Bay, Sandy Neck, and all the way to Provincetown Light. The keeping room (living room) has a large Count Rumford fireplace (an efficient, shallow fireplace designed by a master craftsman). The dining room is furnished with a long table where scrumptious breakfasts are served. There is no air conditioning, but hopefully your visit will be at a time when the gentle breezes of the Cape blow through the inn. *Directions:* From Boston follow Route 3 to the Sagamore Bridge to Route 6 then take exit 6 to Route 132 north to Route 6A. Turn right on Route 6A to Barnstable Village, going through the only traffic light and past the church. Turn left onto Powder Hill Road and into the first driveway on the left.

COBB'S COVE INN
Innkeepers: Evelyn Chester & Henri-Jean Studley
Powder Hill Road, P.O. Box 208
Barnstable Village, MA 02630
Tel & fax: (508) 362-9356
6 rooms, Double: $149–$189
Open all year
Credit cards: all major
Restaurant: none
Handicap room: none
www.karenbrown.com/ne/cobbscoveinn.html

The Charles Street Inn is beautifully located at the foot of Beacon Hill, that historic district where the Colonial merchants first built their homes. It is within walking distance of all that you may want to explore in downtown Boston. Its front is on busy Charles Street, so I prefer the rooms at the back, which are both larger and quieter, overlooking the very private area of Mount Vernon Square (the Oliver Wendell Holmes room has great views onto this). The guestrooms have all been totally redecorated in a Victorian style unique to each room. Beds are either queen or king and either four-posters or canopied. Each room has a sitting area where you can have your Continental breakfast, if you choose not to go the reception area on the ground floor. The rooms' amenities are superb: wood-burning marble fireplaces, air conditioning, extra-large whirlpool tubs, in-room mini-bars, two-line phone service with voice mail, high-speed internet access, cable TVs and VCRs, AM/FM/CD systems, under-counter refrigerators and ice makers, microwaves, and coffee makers. Baths have granite counters, white tile, and cherry-wood cabinets. In the John Singer Sargent room there are two double beds and an elegant writing desk, with French blue and cream chintz dominating the decor. There is a new elevator providing easy access to the rooms. *Directions*: From the west take Storrow Drive into Boston, then turn onto Charles Street to inn. From the airport take the Sumner Tunnel to Route 93 north to Storrow Drive and then take the Charles Street exit.

THE CHARLES STREET INN
Innkeepers: Louise Venden & Sally Deane
94 Charles Street
Boston, MA 02114-4643
Tel: (617) 314-8900 or (888) 877-8900
Fax: (617) 371-0009
9 rooms, Double: $200–$330
Open all year, Credit cards: all major
Restaurant: none
Handicap room
www.karenbrown.com/ne/charlesstreetinn.html

In the heart of Boston on Boylston Street stands The Lenox, recently renovated by the Saunders family into a very chic place for you to stay while you are visiting the many attractions of Boston. It is located in the heart of Boylston and Newbury Streets' shopping and art galleries, which could keep you busy for days. Copley Place and the Prudential Center are within a couple of blocks. This is a large hotel with 212 guestrooms, each with private bathroom, and since the hotel was recently refurbished, the rooms are especially attractive. One of the rooms I visited had a corner fireplace, wonderfully comfortable seating, and two queen beds. It was decorated in tones of taupe and had flowered drapes, which pulled across the windows in the evening. This is a full-service hotel offering amenities such as voice mail, in-room fax machines, phones with modem ports, laundry service, and conference facilities. Anago is the formal dining room but there is also a pub serving lighter food in a casual setting and room service is available. The Upstairs Café serves breakfast daily. The hotel has the bonus of an on-site exercise room. *Directions*: Take I-93 into Boston, exiting at the signs to Copley Square. Turn right at Beacon Street for four blocks and then take a left on Exeter Street and The Lenox is four blocks down on the right.

THE LENOX
Owner: Saunders Hotel Group
710 Boylston Street
Boston, MA 02116
Tel: (617) 536-5300 or (800) 225-7676
Fax: (617) 236-0351
E-mail: info@lenoxhotel.com
212 rooms, Double: $308–$598*,
  *Breakfast not included
Open all year
Credit cards: all major
Restaurant: all meals
Handicap room

Sea captains' homes fill the landscape in this lovely Cape Cod town. The Captain Freeman Inn was home to one of those merchants whose wealth came from the rich clipper trade in the late 1800s and a picture of his ship, the *Kingfisher*, hangs in the entry hall. Elegant architectural details are everywhere in this building—ornate plaster moldings, wood floors in intricate patterns, a commanding center staircase, and a parlor with marble fireplace and floor-to-ceiling windows. There are traditional and luxury guestrooms, all wonderful and all air-conditioned. The luxury rooms have queen canopy beds, fireplaces, cable TV/VCRs, and refrigerators, with spa tubs in the bathrooms. Among the traditional rooms it is hard to choose between the cozy bedroom with dark paneling, queen bed, and hand-sewn canopy and the queen bedroom with the pine four-poster and lace canopy. Some rooms can accommodate an additional person. The inn has its own swimming pool and there are croquet and badminton courts on the 1½-acre lawn. An elegant wrap-around porch is a perfect spot to rock away the hours with iced tea or lemonade. A short walk from the inn will bring you to the local beach. The Captain Freeman Inn has winter weekend cooking classes hosted by one of the chef/owners who three times a year also teach a course on innkeeping. *Directions*: Leave Route 6 at exit 10, taking Route 124 towards Brewster. At the end of Route 124, go right on Route 6A, then left on Breakwater to the first driveway on the left.

THE CAPTAIN FREEMAN INN
Innkeepers: Carol & Tom Edmondson
15 Breakwater Road
Brewster, MA 02631
Tel: (508) 896-7581 or (800) 843-4664
Fax: (508) 896-7481
E-mail: visitus@capecod.net
12 rooms, Double: $145–$250
Open all year
Credit cards: all major
Restaurant: none
Handicap room: none

Situated on the outskirts of Cambridge and Boston, A Cambridge House has 15 bedrooms, each with private bath and all elegantly furnished with premier fabrics and charming decor. While the rooms are not large, they provide everything the visitor might want, and most especially that cozy feeling of home. The four-poster beds have down comforters and an assortment of pillows and each room has comfortable seating, a telephone, voice mail, and color TV. Many of the rooms have fireplaces. The flowered or patterned wallpapers are exquisite and in some rooms the matching fabric has been used on the bed canopy. A full buffet breakfast is served in either of the two equally beautiful living rooms and in the evening, hors d'oeuvres and beverages are offered to guests returning from the day's activities. The inn provides complimentary parking, although it's not on the inn property. Public transportation is the key to getting around Boston and Cambridge: it's easy and convenient and you'll be glad to leave your car while you explore the endless array of things to do in the Boston area. Logan Airport is about 20 minutes from the inn. *Directions:* The inn may be reached by car, taxi, or bus and has very detailed directions, which are given to every guest. Please contact the hotel directly for written directions.

A CAMBRIDGE HOUSE
Innkeeper: Ellen Riley
2218 Massachusetts Ave
Cambridge, MA 02140-1846
Tel: (617) 491-6300 or (800) 232-9989
Fax: (617) 868-2848
E-mail: InnACH@aol.com
15 rooms, Double: $149–$275
Open all year
Credit cards: all major
Restaurant: none
Handicap room
www.karenbrown.com/ne/acambridgehouse.html

Captain Hiram Harding, a packet skipper in the 1800s, built this home in 1839, and the inn's very individual rooms are named after his family and the ships he sailed. This inn is an elegant compound with 17 guestrooms clustered around a handsome Greek Revival home. The common areas are attractively furnished with antiques and the dining-room sun porch is surrounded by floor-to-ceiling windows giving views into the delightful gardens with their lawns, mature plantings, and flowering shrubs. Breakfast is served here with sterling silver and fine china on linen-covered tables. Each bedroom is individually decorated and many will remind you of the cozy feeling of Colonial times with their beamed ceilings, fireplaces, and queen or king beds with antique bedposts. Many of the rooms have original random-width pine floors, which add to the charm of the decor. All rooms have private baths, a few have spa tubs, and several have private decks. I loved my room with its dark paneling, a massive king bed that I had to get into using a small set of steps, and a fireplace with two wing chairs that just begged me to sit and read. Remember times gone by when life was simpler; think of all the amenities you could possibly desire in an inn; dream of gardens and bikes and croquet—you will find them all at The Captain's House Inn. *Directions:* Leave Route 6 at exit 11 south, taking Route 137 to Route 28. Turn left and drive about 3 miles to the rotary. Follow the rotary around to the left (still on Route 28) toward Orleans. The inn is ½ mile along on the left.

THE CAPTAIN'S HOUSE INN
Innkeepers: Jan & Dave McMaster
369–377 Old Harbor Road
Chatham, MA 02633
Tel: (508) 945-0127 or (800) 315-0728
Fax: (508) 945-0866
E-mail: info@captainshouseinn.com
14 rooms, 3 suites, Double: $165–$275, Suite: $225–$375
Open all year, Credit cards: all major
Restaurant: none
Handicap room
www.karenbrown.com/ne/thecaptainshouseinn.html

The historic town of Concord is one of those very special New England towns that draw the visitor in to share their past and to experience their welcoming charm. Here you find a quaint village with interesting shops, lovely old homes lining the streets, a magnificent white church set back on the green, and on the far edge of the green a landmark inn— Concord's Colonial Inn, built in 1716 as a family residence. It became a hotel in 1889, providing cozy bars with fireplaces, a choice of dining rooms, and comfortably decorated bedrooms, as it still does today. Several wings have been added to the original structure, giving 56 bedrooms in the various buildings, including the Cottage and Rebecca's Guest House. The inn reflects all the busyness of a hotel that can accommodate up to 80 for a meeting or a private function but there are many places where the guest can find a quiet place to sit and enjoy the very special warmth that comes from a house that has lived so long. The bedrooms have all the amenities expected by the business traveler: voice mail, fax, data ports on the phones, and laundry service. Suites with kitchenettes are perfect for extended stays. *Directions:* Concord is easily reached by taking Route 2 from downtown Boston or from the circumferential Route 128. Signs on Route 2 lead you into Concord and the inn sits at the far end of the village green.

CONCORD'S COLONIAL INN
Innkeeper: Gergen Demisch
48 Monument Square
Concord, MA 01742
Tel: (978) 369-9200 or (800) 370-9200
Fax: (978) 371-1533
E-mail: colonial@concordscolonialinn.com
46 rooms, 6 suites, 4 guesthouse suites
Double: $135–$225*, Suite: $155–$225*,
  Guesthouse Suite: $200–$475*, *Breakfast not included
Open all year
Credit cards: all major
Restaurant: all meals
Handicap room

The town of Concord is steeped in the history of the founding of the American Colonies and in the battles with Britain that led to independence. The Hawthorne Inn, built in 1870 and situated on land that once belonged to Ralph Waldo Emerson, the Alcotts, and Nathaniel Hawthorne, is within easy walking distance of many of the town's points of historical interest. The inn is nicely set among many trees and gardens, which I found to be very welcoming. The bedrooms are named after famous people or places associated with this area—for example, Emerson, Alcott, Walden, and Sleepy Hollow—and the books in the rooms continue the theme. Flowered wallpapers, queen canopy beds, and hand-sewn quilts make the bedrooms very comfortable. They are not large but they provide all you'll want after a day of touring the history-filled countryside. Children are welcomed and if yours are interested in history, it would be hard to think of a better place to stay. The owners are art aficionados and have hung the walls with an eclectic collection of contemporary art. Continental breakfast, the only meal served, offers fresh fruit, juice, home-baked breads, and either a selection of teas or the inn's own blend of coffee. The innkeepers have prepared a week's program of things for you to do while visiting the area—follow their suggestions for a memorable and educational vacation. *Directions:* Take exit 30 (Route 2A West) from Routes 128 & 95 and bear right at the fork toward Concord for 1-2/10 miles. The inn is directly across the road from Hawthorne's home.

HAWTHORNE INN
Innkeepers: Gregory Burch & Marilyn Mudry
462 Lexington Road
Concord, MA 01742
Tel: (978) 369-5610, Fax: (978) 287-4949
E-mail: inn@concordmass.com
7 rooms, Double: $200–$275
Open all year, Credit cards: all major
Restaurant: none
Handicap room: none
www.karenbrown.com/ne/hawthorneinn.html

Visiting historic Deerfield is dropping into the heart of a 330-year-old New England village, with historic homes lining its wide Main Street. Fourteen of the village's old houses hold more than 20,000 objects—furniture, silver, glass, ceramics, and textiles— made or used in America between 1650 and 1850. The classic 1884 Deerfield Inn is the centerpiece of this village and its 23 guestrooms are all named after people associated with the village's history. Horatio Alger, room 141, has pastel window draperies inspired by a book on period valances. The wallpaper picks up the floral, romantic theme and the mahogany king-sized sleigh bed has an inviting patchwork quilt across the foot. Many of the bedrooms, with the vibrant paintwork typical of the Federal period in New England, have faux testers and antique four-posters. Others are reminiscent of the English settlers that first made Deerfield their home. Everett House, for example, room 145, has a delicate English window treatment and sunny wallpaper in greens and warm yellows, with cheerful throw pillows on the cannonball bed. I stayed in a smaller room with a queen canopy bed, comfortable antique chairs, and good lighting for reading. All rooms have private baths, telephones, TVs, and individual climate controls. The award-winning restaurant serves American cuisine, the terrace café provides light meals, and the tavern offers local and international brews and a supper menu. *Directions*: Going north on I-91 take exit 24, exit 25 going south. Deerfield Village is just off Routes 5 and 10 north.

DEERFIELD INN
Innkeepers: Jane & Karl Sabo
81 Old Main Street
Deerfield, MA 01342-0305
Tel: (413) 774-5587 or (800) 926-3865
Fax: (413) 775-7221
E-mail: kbg@deerfieldinn.com
23 rooms, Double: $188–$255
Closed Christmas, Credit cards: all major
Restaurant: all meals
Handicap room
www.karenbrown.com/ne/deerfieldinn.html

Halfway along the length of Cape Cod an "elbow" marks the start of the unspoiled, unhurried, and absolutely beautiful Outer Cape. With 40 miles of National Seashore, this is a very special place, with none of the tourist activities usually associated with the Cape. Equally special is The Whalewalk Inn, an 1830s whaling master's home that has been meticulously restored to provide 16 beautifully decorated and spacious guestrooms, each with private bath, in the main house and the recently built carriage house. The rooms are just wonderful with their charm, sophisticated country decor, and individual palettes of colors. It would be hard to find a favorite here but I loved the king-sized bedroom with its own private entrance and a fireplace. Carolyn is one of those innkeepers who is always looking for the right painting or art object to go in each room. The Whalewalk Inn sits on a street of Colonial homes that beckons you to walk down to the beach. When the sun goes down the inn glows with the lights and candles in its windows. A lot of love has gone into the creation of The Whalewalk and the owners are also passionate about the preparation of food: the breakfasts served here are ones that you'll remember for a long time. *Directions:* Take Route 6 to the Orleans rotary, then the Rock Harbor exit off the rotary. Turn left on Rock Harbor Road and right on Bridge Road.

THE WHALEWALK INN
Innkeepers: Carolyn & Richard Smith
220 Bridge Road
Eastham, MA 02642
Tel: (508) 255-0617 or (800) 440-1281
Fax: 508-240-0017
E-mail: whalewak@capecod.net
11 rooms, 5 suites
Double: $160–$300
Open April to December & winter weekends
Credit cards: all major
Restaurant: none
Handicap room
www.karenbrown.com/ne/thewhalewalkinn.html

The Charlotte Inn in Edgartown is a formal and beautifully decorated inn with lovely antiques and much original art—a lot of which is for sale. As with many of the inns on Martha's Vineyard, this historic home was built in the last half of the 19th century and once belonged to a sea captain. Brick paths lead you to lovely gardens and cozy places to relax: there's an especially beautiful rose garden with a lattice, which can be seen from several of the inn's rooms. Next door in the carriage house you find some of the inn's twenty-three bedrooms and two suites, all of which are luxurious and have every possible amenity. Each has that quality and feeling of a room you've been away from and to which you have just come home. The formal dining room, L'Etoile, celebrates the best of the French style of cuisine while making use of local ingredients. Dining is also available in the glass-paned conservatory or outdoors on a terrace where you are surrounded by plants. This is not an inn where you wander through with sandy feet from the beach, but rather an inn where you celebrate a special occasion in a meticulously orchestrated setting. *Directions:* You reach the island of Martha's Vineyard by plane from New York or Boston or seasonally by car ferry from Woods Hole or passenger ferry from Hyannis or New Bedford.

THE CHARLOTTE INN
Innkeepers: Paula & Gery Conover
Manager: Carol Read
South Summer Street
(Martha's Vineyard)
Edgartown, MA 02539
Tel: (508) 627-4751 or (508) 627-4151
Fax: (508) 627-4652
23 rooms, 2 suites, Double: $295–$750
Open all year
Credit cards: all major
Restaurant: dinner only
Handicap room: none

Take an estate high on a hill belonging to the owners' grandparents, surrounded with gorgeous, century-old homes and placed within walking distance of everything in town; add major refurbishment to an already interesting Greek Revival home; mix traditional decor with modern; hire an artist to faux paint; plan cozy common rooms, a living room with views of the garden, and lovely dining rooms; throw in a fitness center and a conference facility; add an eclectic collection of art—and you have created a fabulous sanctuary on Martha's Vineyard. Of course, the guestrooms provide every amenity you could possibly wish for. One of my favorite rooms is tucked up under the eaves with a white-painted four-poster bed, painted bedside tables and bureau, and chairs with flower-print fabrics. Enjoy a wonderful breakfast, afternoon tea with freshly baked scones, and a frosty pitcher of lemonade on the wrap around porch, and then, if you've caught that bass, the inn will grill it for you and friends at a private dinner party. The inn's staff may suggest activities to keep you busy—fishing, walking the beaches, visiting galleries, kayaking—or will direct you to a chair by the fire in the living room. *Directions:* You reach the island of Martha's Vineyard by plane from New York or Boston or by car ferry from Woods Hole or seasonally by passenger ferry from Hyannis or New Bedford.

HOB KNOB INN
Innkeeper: Erin Mansell
128 Main Street, P.O. Box 239
(Martha's Vineyard)
Edgartown, MA 02539
Tel: (508) 627-9510 or (800) 676-2723
Fax: (508) 627-4560
E-mail: hobknob@vineyard.net
20 rooms, Double: $200–$525
Open all year, Credit cards: all major
Restaurant: none
Handicap room

The architecture of this inn is an interesting combination of Colonial and Greek Revival styles but it's what the owners have done to this property that makes it so very special. Built in the 1850s as a sea captain's home, it has been transformed into an inn with a blend of traditional and contemporary elegance, which makes your stay a memorable one. Decor in the public rooms is informal and comfortable, and has been designed by an owner with an artist's eye. I was especially interested in the artwork, a mix of old and new, of paintings, prints, and photography. I particularly liked the photos of beach, sea grass, and dunes. There's a lovely sunny room for breakfast and a warm and cozy common room for the evening. Plantings of sea grass in the garden and artfully placed sculpture make for an interesting twist on the normal garden. The front porch gives you a place from which to watch the ebb and flow of Edgartown. Guestrooms are freshly decorated, many have fireplaces, and several have porches or decks that look over the delightful garden. Showers, beach towels, and luggage storage are available so that after you've checked out you can go to the beach till ferry time. A courtesy car is available on a shared-use basis for exploring the more distant parts of the island. *Directions*: : You reach the island of Martha's Vineyard by plane from New York or Boston or by car ferry from Woods Hole or seasonally by passenger ferry from Hyannis or New Bedford.

POINT WAY INN
Innkeepers: Claudia Miller & John Glendon
Main Street & Pease's Point Way
(Martha's Vineyard)
Edgartown, MA 02539
Tel: (888) 711-6633, Fax: (508) 627-3338
E-mail: pointwayinn@vineyard.net
12 rooms, Double: $125–$375
Open all year, Credit cards: all major
Restaurant: none
Handicap room
www.karenbrown.com/ne/pointwayinn.html

Mostly Hall was built in 1849 by Captain Albert Nye as a wedding present for his southern bride to equal the charm of her New Orleans home and it's the only plantation-style home on Cape Cod. Its name came from a visiting child who, upon entering the building, exclaimed, "Why mama, it's mostly hall!" And so it is. It also provides the grand feeling found only in homes that have exceptionally high ceilings. When I visited, a renovation project was nearing completion and the walls were being faux painted to give this inn a distinctive European feeling. Bedrooms also enjoy high ceilings and each has its own private bath. The European-style breakfast consists of a wide variety of cheeses, cold cuts, caviar, products from Provence, and freshly baked pastries. There's a wonderful enclosed widow's walk on top of the inn where you can relax and look out in every direction. La Maison Cappellari at Mostly Hall is situated on the village green in the appealing coastside town of Falmouth on the lower Cape and makes a perfect stopover for travelers en route to or from the islands of Martha's Vineyard and Nantucket. *Directions*: From Boston take Route 3 south to the Bourne Bridge onto Cape Cod, then Route 28 south to Falmouth. The inn is located just off the village green, with the driveway between granite posts.

LA MAISON CAPPELLARI AT MOSTLY HALL
Innkeepers: Christina & Bodgan Simcic
27 West Main Street
Falmouth, MA 02540
Telephone: (508) 548-3786
Fax: (508) 548-5778
E-mail: mostlyhall@aol.com
6 rooms, Double: $195–$240
Open March to December
Credit cards: all major
Restaurant: none
Handicap room: none

Travel 120 miles west of Boston and discover Blantyre, a Tudor-style mansion built in 1902 and set on a hill on 85 acres of spectacular Berkshire countryside. Replicating a grand Scottish manor, Blantyre is indeed a step back into a time of elegance and gracious living, bringing to the visitor a world of serene European ambiance, calm, courtesy, charm, and cuisine. From the main hall with its immense fireplace and massive, ornate furniture, a sweeping oak staircase leads you up to eight of the bedrooms. I fell in love with the grandeur of The Paterson Suite with its king mahogany four-poster bed sitting beneath exquisite flower prints, large sitting area with fireplace, and two bathrooms. An additional twelve guestrooms are found in the carriage house and there are three cottages. In the carriage house Wyndhurst has a queen four-poster bed with lovely lace coverings and French windows opening onto the expansive lawns. Several rooms have fireplaces and all provide every luxurious amenity. The conservatory, originally used for plants brought in from the greenhouse, is now the setting for breakfasts, lunch, and dinner. There's also a covered terrace overlooking the south lawn where you can have lunch or an informal meeting. *Directions*: Leave I-90 at exit 2 in Lee and take Route 20 west 3 miles to the entrance to Blantyre.

BLANTYRE
Director: Roderick Anderson
Blantyre Road, P.O. Box 995
Lenox, MA 01240
Tel: (413) 637-3556, Fax: (413) 637-4282
E-mail: hide@blantyre.com
12 rooms, 11 suites
Double: $320–$800
Open May 4 to November 4
Credit cards: all major
Restaurant: all meals
Handicap room

Marblehead is one of the great sailing capitals of the world today as it was in centuries past when tall-masted schooners carried the products of a new nation to and from Europe and the Far East. 17th- and 18th-century homes crowd the narrow, winding streets of one of the most popular places to visit on the New England coast. Within this historic district you find a 21-room, elegantly decorated inn whose warmth of welcome immediately makes you feel as though you have stepped back in time while enjoying all the amenities of the 21st century. I loved the flowered wallpapers used in the front hallway, in the dining room, and in the parlors. Guestrooms have king and queen beds, some with canopies, some have fireplaces, some have decks or patios, some have Jacuzzis, but all provide a cozy ambiance and fine furnishings. Enjoy the stunning view from the rooftop walk from which you can see the famous Marblehead light. Surprisingly in a town where houses crowd the streets, there is a lovely garden and a heated swimming pool, which offers a refreshing respite after a day of exploring the town's shops, galleries, and restaurants. This is a formal inn but one of such comfort that you will instantly feel the warm welcome of the inn's staff and become yet another of its centuries of houseguests. Breakfast is served in the large dining room at a lovely long mahogany table. *Directions:* From Boston take Route 1A north to Route 129 east to Marblehead. Take the first right after the Texaco station: the inn is 1/8 mile down on the right

THE HARBOR LIGHT INN
Innkeepers: Suzanne & Peter Conway
58 Washington Street
Marblehead, MA 01945
Tel: (781) 631-2186, Fax: (781) 631-2216
E-mail: hli@shore.net
20 rooms, 3 suites
Double: $110–$165, Suite: $150–$275
Open all year, Credit cards: all major
Restaurant: none
Handicap room: none
www.karenbrown.com/ne/harborlightinn.html

The stately 1838 Greek Revival family home of whaling-ship captain Uriah Russell has been transformed into a very elegant inn in the town of Nantucket on the very charming island of Nantucket. In 1997 this inn was completely restored and now the common rooms and bedrooms are furnished with a mix of authentic and reproduction antiques that give the inn a great deal of charm and warmth. Bedrooms have handmade four-poster beds with canopies, goose-down comforters with flower-print covers, Oriental carpets, and marble bathrooms. Each of the very attractively and elegantly furnished rooms has a private bath, air conditioning, TV (hidden in a reproduction highboy), and telephone with data port. Breakfast, consisting of freshly squeezed orange juice, fresh fruit, hot and cold cereals, and pastries, is served in the dining room or on the lovely garden terrace where you can enjoy the bubbling fountain. I loved the commercial espresso machine from which you can choose a cappuccino, café latte, or an espresso. One of the many wonderful things about Nantucket is that it is an easy walk from the ferry docks to almost everything there is to do and every place there is to stay. *Directions:* From the steamship ferry landing walk up Broad Street, turn left on Center Street, then second right onto Hussey Street. From the Hy-Line landing walk up Main Street, turn right on Center Street, then third left onto Hussey Street.

THE PINEAPPLE INN
Innkeepers: Caroline & Bob Taylor
10 Hussey Street
(Nantucket Island)
Nantucket, MA 02554
Tel: (508) 228-9992, Fax: (508) 325-6051
E-mail: info@pineappleinn.com
12 rooms, Double: $160–$295
Open late April to early December
Credit cards: all major
Restaurant: none, Handicap room: none
www.karenbrown.com/ne/thepineappleinn.html

There is a magic to being on the island of Nantucket and in the heart of its principal town. Stay here in a warm and cozy post-and-beam guesthouse with innkeepers who make you feel like family and it's difficult to imagine life much better. Seven Sea Street, newly built in traditional style, is appointed with early-American furnishings combined with all the modern conveniences. The 11 guestrooms have queen beds with fishnet canopies, TVs, telephones, small refrigerators, and all those other amenities including air conditioning that make your stay so pleasant. I stayed in a simply but comfortably furnished small suite with a separate living room. Puddy, the inn cat, made it quite evident that he intended to spend the night in my room—cats do know cat people! There's a relaxing common room with a pot-bellied stove and a dining room with a long table on which breakfast is served. It is a perfect spot to linger over a second cup of fresh coffee and talk with other guests. A Continental breakfast is available in your room if you don't feel like socializing in the mornings. From the inn it's just a few blocks' walk to Main Street with all its fabulous architecture—don't miss the Three Bricks mansions built by a merchant for his three sons, and the upscale shops and galleries. *Directions:* By air from Boston, New York, and Providence. By ferry from Woods Hole, New Bedford, and Hyannis—the inn is three minutes from the dock.

SEVEN SEA STREET
Innkeepers: Mary & Matthew Parker
7 Sea Street
(Nantucket Island)
Nantucket, MA 02554
Tel: (508) 228-3577, Fax: (508) 228-3578
E-mail: seast7@nantucket.net
9 rooms, 2 suites, Double: $175–$295
Open all year
Credit cards: all major
Restaurant: none
Handicap room: none
www.karenbrown.com/ne/sevenseastreet.html

Between the towns of Orleans and Chatham there is a delightful two-room bed and breakfast inn set high on a hill overlooking a wooded ravine. Within its 5 acres Morgan's Way provides a tranquil setting for those who want to truly be away from it all. This architect-designed contemporary Cape-style house is the home of your hosts while also providing private guest accommodations including a spacious living area on the second floor with a wood-burning stove, TV/VCR, library, and small refrigerator. Tall windows look onto the beauty of the surrounding woodlands and many gardens. Sliding doors open to a small deck and spiral stairs leading down to a heated pool (available from May through September). The two large bedrooms are attractively furnished with queen beds and comfortable reading chairs and each room has its own bathroom (one is two steps down the hall). A full gourmet breakfast is provided each morning in the owner's dining room. Beside the pool is an especially delightful self-catering house that accommodates two people and is let on a weekly basis. If you plan to be in this area for a week or so, I'd suggest that you look into the availability of this charming cottage. *Directions:* Take Route 6 from Sagamore Bridge to exit 12 then turn right onto Route 6A. At the first light turn right and right at the next light onto Route 28. Drive 1 mile to Morgan's Way.

MORGAN'S WAY BED & BREAKFAST
Innkeepers: Page McMahan & Will Joy
9 Morgan's Way
Orleans, MA 02653
Tel: (508) 255-0831, Fax: (508) 255-0831
E-mail: morgnway@capecod.net
2 rooms, 1 housekeeping cottage
Double: $125–$129, Cottage: $900 weekly
Open all year, 2-night minimum, 3 on holiday weekends
Credit cards: none accepted
Restaurant: none
Handicap room: none
www.karenbrown.com/ne/morgansway.html

Perched on the ledges above the ocean about an hour north of Boston airport sits the Yankee Clipper Inn, its twenty-six guest accommodations in four buildings nicely separated from one another by landscaping and by the rolling terrain. Most of the rooms have views of the ocean through large picture windows, with comfortable chairs positioned for watching the ever-changing scenery of the seashore. Bedrooms are simply furnished with queen, king, or twin beds, some canopied, and all have private baths. Six rooms have Jacuzzis. Of the guest accommodations, two are termed suites and there is also one three-bedroom villa. A heated saltwater swimming pool is available on the property and nearby you find tennis, golf, hiking, fishing, biking, and summer theatre. Rockport is a charming village with galleries, antique shops, and restaurants as well as a large community of artists who spend the summer there. The inn has a very good restaurant with fabulous ocean views, the Veranda, which features New England gourmet cuisine. This would be a great stopover for anyone headed for Maine and the upper New England coast. There are various mid-week and special-activity package plans, which offer very good value for money. *Directions*: Take Route 128 north to Cape Ann through Gloucester. Turn left on Route 127 for about 3 miles to Rockport's Five Corners and a sign for Pigeon Cove, where the road makes a sharp left. Turn left and continue for 1-2/10 miles to the inn.

YANKEE CLIPPER INN
Innkeepers: Barbara & Bob Ellis
96 Granite Street, P.O. Box 2399
Rockport, MA 01966
Tel: (978) 546-3407 or (800) 545-3699
Fax: (978) 546-9730
E-mail: info@yankeeclipperinn.com
24 rooms, 2 suites, 1 3-bedroom villa
Double: $119–$319, Villa: $2,500 weekly
Open Mar. to Dec. 15, Credit cards: all major
Restaurant: breakfast and dinner
Handicap room: none

In the center of the lovely town of Sandwich, one of the gateways to Cape Cod, you will find the Daniel Webster Inn. This is a full-service inn with 54 guestrooms, a cozy tavern, an informal dining room with a large fireplace, and a formal dining room with a glass wall looking into an enclosed courtyard and garden. These are especially attractive spots in which to pause in the day's activities to enjoy both the ambiance and the food. In the tavern the food focuses on scrumptious appetizers, a variety of salads, burgers, sandwiches, and, in the evening, a number of entrees. If you prefer a more formal meal, head for the restaurant where the emphasis is on fresh seafood, with plenty of additional choices for meat lovers. An extensive wine list is available. All guestrooms are most attractively furnished. I was in one of the newer rooms with a fireplace, canopy bed, luxurious spa tub, and heated marble floor in the bathroom. In the off season there is an expanded Continental breakfast, while breakfast in season is served à la carte. Room service is available. *Directions:* From Boston take Route 3 south to Route 6 then leave at exit 2. Turn left on Route 130 for 2 miles, going right at the fork—the inn is on the left.

DANIEL WEBSTER INN
Innkeepers: The Catania Family
149 Main Street
Sandwich, MA 02563
Tel: (508) 888-3622 or (800) 444-3566
Fax: (508) 888-5156
E-mail: dwi@capecod.net
37 rooms, 17 suites
Double: $119–$349*, Suite $230–$425*,
  *Breakfast not included
Closed Christmas
Credit cards: all major
Restaurant: all meals, Sunday brunch
Handicap room
www.karenbrown.com/ne/danielwebsterinn.html

The Isaiah Jones Homestead, built in 1849, has many wonderful antiques of the sort that I would just love to have in my own home. However, my envy extends beyond the furniture, for I would love to install the graceful curved staircase leading from the front hall to the bedrooms in my home in California. The gathering room has an 11-foot ceiling and crown molding reminiscent of the Victorian era in which the home was built. Toast your toes by the fireplace and relax with a cup of tea nestled by the window. Breakfasts, served by candlelight at the mahogany dining table, are welcoming, with the early-morning aroma of freshly baked breads and delicious entrees. All the bedrooms have queen-size beds, and five have fireplaces and four have whirlpool tubs. There's a small porch on which you can sit and rock while reading a good book. The location is perfect for walking into the center of the village of Sandwich, to the Glass Museum, the antique shops, and to the restaurants. Sandwich is a great spot for either beginning or ending your trip to Cape Cod as it is located just east of the Sagamore Bridge over the Cape Cod Canal on the north shore of the Cape. *Directions:* Leave Route 6 at exit 2, going left on Route 130. Bear right at the fork for 2/10 mile and the inn is on the left.

ISAIAH JONES HOMESTEAD
Innkeepers: Jan & Doug Kapper
165 Main Street
Sandwich, MA 02563
Tel: (508) 888-9115 or (800) 526-1625
Fax: (508) 888-9645
E-mail: info@isaiahjones.com
5 rooms, 2 suites, Double: $99–$185
Open all year
Credit cards: all major
Restaurant: none
Handicap room: none

Opening the door of this 1835 Greek Revival inn with its 1785 origins, I was enveloped by the smell of cookies baking in the kitchen. This made it hard to concentrate on looking at the living and dining rooms but among the features that did stand out were the beehive oven fireplace and the spectacular moldings found throughout the inn. The common rooms are attractively decorated and there's a great fireplace in the New England tradition. There are ten bedrooms with a combination of kings, queens, and twins, each with its own bath. One room has a pencil-post king bed, hardwood floors, blue-flowered wallpaper, and comfortable chairs; a room under the eaves with dormers also has hardwood floors, braided oval rugs, and a red, white, and blue quilt on the queen bed. At the end of a day of enjoying the many activities in this area (antiquing, music, shopping, the Norman Rockwell Museum, and all the sports you can name), you can return to the inn for a cup of tea and a sweet. Afterwards you can dine in one of the many wonderful nearby restaurants. (The innkeepers will prepare dinner for parties of ten or more guests.) A scrumptious full breakfast is served in the dining room, with its tables set for four and Hitchcock-style chairs. *Directions:* From New York take the Taconic Parkway to Route 23 east then drive 13 miles to the inn on the right. From the Massachusetts Turnpike take exit 2 to Route 202 to Route 7 south, then Route 23 west to the inn on the left.

THE WEATHERVANE INN
Innkeepers: Maxine & Jeffrey Lome
Route 23, Box 388
South Egremont, MA 01258
Tel: (413) 528-9580 or (800) 528-9580
Fax: (413) 528-1713
E-mail: innkeeper@weathervaneinn.com
8 rooms, 2 suites, Double $115–$245
Open all year
Credit cards: all major
Restaurant: none
Handicap room: none

As you stand at the door of the Captain Farris House and see the National Historic Register plaque, you know somehow that you are in for a real treat and when you get inside you are not disappointed. Although relatively new to innkeeping, the hospitable Bronsteins provide accommodations you won't want to leave. The cozy parlor is perfect for relaxing after a day of sightseeing, the dining room is stunning with its long table, corner cabinet, and sideboard, and the informal garden breakfast room with its large skylight brings the outdoors in to you. The bedrooms, located in the main house and in a small building next door, are wonderful, with crisp, white linens, cable TV, and VCR. All but one of the bathrooms have Jacuzzi tubs and showers. Some rooms have sundecks or private porches and most have private entrances. Suites have fireplaces in the living rooms and a large bedroom, and there is one two-bedroom suite with a spacious living room and a dining room equipped with microwave. The Phoebe White Suite was my favorite with its spacious living room, fireplace, and bedroom with a queen canopy bed. Its bathroom has a two-person Jacuzzi and there's a sundeck to boot. Breakfast features a freshly baked pastry, fresh fruit, and a hot entree. *Directions:* From Boston take I-93 south to Route 3 south, crossing the Sagamore Bridge to Route 6 toward Hyannis. Leave at exit 8 onto Station Avenue for 2-1/10 miles to the yield sign. Continue straight to the intersection of Route 28, cross over, and the inn is about one block down on the right.

CAPTAIN FARRIS HOUSE
Innkeepers: Patricia & Stephen Bronstein
308 Old Main Street
South Yarmouth, MA 02664
Tel: (508) 760-2818 or (800) 350-9477
Fax: (508) 398-1262
E-mail: mail@captainfarris.com
6 rooms, 4 suites, Double: $95–$225
Open all year
Credit cards: all major
Restaurant: none
Handicap room

The Inn at Stockbridge is a large turn-of-the-century domain situated down a winding driveway on 12 acres of land with so many trees that I felt I had entered my own private estate. You arrive at a columned porch and on the other side of the front door is a very large welcoming hall flanked by the dining room on one side and the gracious living room on the other. The living room, where wine is served in the afternoon, is comfortably furnished and reading by the fire here is a real pleasure. The inn's 12 guestrooms are in both the main house and the cottage house. Blagdon, the original master bedroom, decorated in soft shades of yellow, has a spacious sitting area in front of the fireplace and a lovely two-poster king bed. The Provence Room, a spacious king-bedded room with red and white toile, a gas fireplace, and TV/VCR, has a definite French flavor. If rocking on a porch is your thing, then the Garden Room off the library is just the place for you. The Inn at Stockbridge prides itself on its breakfasts, formal affairs by candlelight, and Alice loves to share her breakfast recipes with guests. The inn is close to so many things to do that you'll have trouble deciding between the antiquing, the music festivals, the Norman Rockwell Museum, and a variety of sports. Guests can also enjoy the inn's swimming pool. *Directions:* Take the Massachusetts Turnpike to Exit 2, drive west on Route 102 to Route 7 north, then go 1-2/10 miles to the inn on the right. From New York take the Taconic Parkway to Route 23 east and Route 7 north past Stockbridge for 1-2/10 miles.

THE INN AT STOCKBRIDGE
Innkeepers: Alice & Len Schiller
Route 7N, Box 618
Stockbridge, MA 01262
Tel: (413) 298-3337 or (888) 466-7865
Fax: (413) 298-3406
E-mail: innkeeper@stockbridgeinn.com
8 rooms, 4 suites
Double: $125–$255, Suite: $180–$280
Open all year, Credit cards: all major
Restaurant: none, Handicap room
www.karenbrown.com/ne/innatstockbridge.html

The Red Lion Inn dates back to 1773 when it was a small tavern where coaches stopped on their journey between Boston and Albany. Today this inn is an institution: visitors come to experience the setting, the history, the collections, the food, and the ambiance established by generations of hospitality. The owners take pride in changing nothing at all, so all the furniture placed there by earlier owners is probably exactly where it sat a century ago. The floors tilt, the walls are not square, and the furnishings look as if they have been there forever. There are 110 guestrooms, 92 with private baths, all offering the amenities of a quality hostelry. Rooms have antique beds (be sure to specify your choice of queen, king, or twins when you make your reservation), flowered wallpapers, white bedspreads, comfortable seating, and good lighting. Some rooms in the main building, my favorites, look out to the Main Street, while others look out to the several buildings that also house guests. Stockbridge and the Berkshires are rich in festivals of the performing arts—Tanglewood is close by—and fine-art and antique galleries. There is easy access to a wealth of sports and the inn has a pool. Stockbridge is New England at its best, especially in the fall with its glorious foliage in full color. *Directions:* Take I-90 to exit 2 at Lee, then Route 102 west to Main Street, Stockbridge. The inn is on the left.

THE RED LION INN
Owners: The Fitzpatrick Family
Innkeeper: Brooks Bradbury
30 Main Street, P.O. Box 954
Stockbridge, MA 01262
Tel: (413) 298-5545, Fax: (413) 298-5130
E-mail: innkeeper@redlioninn.com
84 rooms, 26 suites, 92 with private bathrooms
Double: $197–$185*, Suite: $197–$400*,
  *Breakfast not included
Open all year, Credit cards: all major
Restaurant: all meals
Handicap room
www.karenbrown.com/ne/redlioninn.html

Sturbridge's location at the intersection of the Massachusetts Turnpike (also referred to as the I-90) and I-84 (between Connecticut and Massachusetts) gives it a perfect position for travelers coming and going throughout New England. How handy that the Tresch family can offer you a selection of places to stay: the Publick House, the Colonel Ebenezer Crafts Inn, and the Country Motor Lodge. Rooms at inns are more our cup of tea but if you do stay at the motor lodge you'll find attractive motel-like rooms with private balconies. Eight pleasant bedrooms are found in the Colonel Ebenezer Crafts Inn. At the Publick House Historic Inn the simply but comfortably furnished rooms (all non-smoking) are part of a building dating back to 1771—this inn has served as a tavern and pub since pre-revolutionary days. In this building you find two different dining rooms: The Dining Room or Ebenezer's Tavern. The Dining Room, where I can attest to the deliciousness of the fabulous lobster pie or the turkey dinner is also where breakfast is served. For a different ambiance but with the same menu for lunch or dinner you might want to settle in Ebenezer's Tavern. Historic Sturbridge Village is just a few minutes' drive away. *Directions:* Located on the green and common in Sturbridge. After leaving I-84 or I-90, follow the signs to the village.

PUBLICK HOUSE HISTORIC INN
Innkeeper: Elisabeth A. Tresch
Route 131
On the Common
Sturbridge, MA 01566
Tel: (508) 347-3313, Fax: (508) 347-1246
E-mail: lodging@ publickhouse.com
Historic Inn: 17 rooms, Crafts Inn: 8 rooms
Double: $120–$160*,
  *Breakfast not included
Open all year
Credit cards: all major
Restaurant: all meals
Handicap room

Longfellow's Wayside Inn, located on 106 acres not far west of Boston, has been open since 1716 and consequently is one of America's oldest operating inns. The original old bar room with its large fireplace, beamed ceiling, and Windsor chairs offers a cozy and welcoming spot for relaxing. The inn is perhaps best known as a restaurant and there are several comfortable dining rooms in various parts of the building. The ten guestrooms are somewhat on the small side, but comfortably furnished, and large enough for a sitting area and private bathroom with tub and shower. A full breakfast is served. As a National Historic site, the inn provides a self-guided walking tour which not only takes you through the rooms of the inn with their individual history but also to the various buildings on the grounds, which include a working grist mill where the whole-wheat flour and cornmeal used in the bakery is ground. The Redstone School house of *Mary Had a Little Lamb* fame was moved to this site years ago and can be toured in seasonable weather. Also on the grounds you find the Martha-Mary Chapel, built in 1940 by Henry Ford in memory of his mother and mother-in-law. This non-denominational chapel is a popular venue for weddings. *Directions:* Just west of Boston, between Boston and Worcester off Route 20. 11 miles west of Route 128 and 7 miles east of Route 495. Follow signs to the inn.

LONGFELLOW'S WAYSIDE INN
Innkeeper: Robert Purrington
Wayside Inn Road
Sudbury, MA 01776
Tel: (978) 443-1776 or (800) 339-1776
Fax: (978) 443-8041
E-mail: longfelo@wayside.org
10 rooms, Double: $120–$145
Closed December 25 & July 4
Credit cards: all major
Restaurant: open daily
Handicap room: none

Beautifully decorated rooms, all with private baths, some with views of the harbor, and a location at the edge of the Main Street within walking distance of the village of Vineyard Haven with its historic homes and its restaurants, make an unbeatable combination. All this in a stately Greek Revival home built in 1840 by the descendents of the settlers of Martha's Vineyard means that this inn is a near-perfect place to be. I thought that Martha's Empire Room with its antique brass half-tester bed draped in blue velvet, a fireplace, and a view of the harbor was especially wonderful, though all the bedrooms in this inn are just lovely. Most of the rooms have fireplaces, all have air conditioning and offer all the amenities, such as stereo/CD/clock-radios. Mountain bikes, tennis rackets (for the local clay courts), and beach chairs are available for your use and a newspaper is left at your door every morning. The dining room, where breakfast is served, is beautiful, the parlor is grand, and there's a porch that is ideal for sitting and people-watching. Stroll one block and you are at the beach, while a few minutes' walk finds you at the ferry. *Directions* You reach the island of Martha's Vineyard by plane or by ferry from various points such as Woods Hole, New Bedford, or Hyannis.

MARTHA'S PLACE
Innkeepers: Richard Alcott & Martin Hicks
114 Main Street
P.O. Box 1182
(Martha's Vineyard)
Vineyard Haven, MA 02568
Tel: (508) 693-0253, Fax: none
E-mail: info@marthasplace.com
6 rooms, Double: $200–$395
Open all year
Credit cards: MC, VS
Restaurant: none
Handicap room: limited

The Thorncroft Inn, whose owners have devoted 20 years to caring for the guests in their inn, have created an environment and a service level that are hard to beat. However, rather than resting on their laurels, they have continued to refine their service and to create new ways to make the guest experience even better. Thought has been given to every detail in the guestrooms, which are wonderful. The twelve rooms and one suite are in two restored buildings furnished with antiques and there's also a separate cottage. Ten of the bedrooms have wood-burning fireplaces and canopied beds. I stayed in a second-floor room that provided me with every comfort in the world, including turn-down service in the evening and coffee and the paper outside my door in the morning. In the inn itself there are family-type common rooms and two dining areas for breakfast and afternoon tea. On the morning I was there, the breakfast of quiche and an array of fresh fruits was so well presented and so colorful that it reminded me of a Gaugin painting. There are lovely paths through the woods and I felt that somehow they too had been designed to add to my relaxation. *Directions:* Take the Steamship Authority ferry from Woods Hole. Turn right at the first stop sign and next right onto Main Street. The inn is 1 mile along on the left.

THORNCROFT INN
Innkeepers: Lynn & Karl Buder
460 Main Street, P.O. Box 1022
(Martha's Vineyard)
Vineyard Haven, MA 02568
Tel: (508) 693-3333 or (800) 332-1236
Fax: (508) 693-5419
E-mail: innkeeper@thorncroft.com
12 rooms, 1 suite, 1 cottage, Double: $180–$500
Open all year, Credit cards: all major
Restaurant: none
Handicap room
www.karenbrown.com/ne/thorncroftinn.html

"It takes a bit of extra effort to get yourself to most very special places"—so says the brochure for The Wauwinet, and it's true. This inn is located on a spit of land jutting into the sea, a ten-minute drive from the town of Nantucket, with a wildlife refuge north of the inn providing many more miles of wonderfully wild isolation. Comprised of a cluster of cottages and the main house with 28 bedrooms, the inn is furnished with tasteful and comfortable seating areas, queen or king beds, and full bathrooms. I found it almost impossible to choose a favorite because all the rooms are spacious, have very attractive artwork, and views either to the bay or the ocean. The ambiance is most definitely homey, like grandmother's house at the beach. The Wauwinet's restaurant is nothing short of fabulous as are its 18,000 bottles of wine. Seafood is always a specialty but there's a full menu for your enjoyment. Paths lead to beaches on either the Atlantic or Nantucket Bay and the grounds have flower gardens, green lawn for sports like croquet, climbing roses, and water views—all enclosed by sand dunes and yet opened by paths leading to sparking waters. Keep busy with sailing, tennis, biking, walking, sea fishing, and bird watching—there is more to do than there are hours in the day for doing it! *Directions:* Travel by ferry from Wood's Hole or Hyannis or by air from major northeast coast cities and from Hyannis and New Bedford.

THE WAUWINET
Innkeepers: Mark Pequignot & Debbie Cleveland
Wauwinet Road, P.O. Box 2580
(Nantucket Island)
Wauwinet, MA 02584
Tel: (508) 228-0145 or (800) 426-8718
Fax: (508) 228-6712
E-mail: email@wauwinet.com
28 rooms, 2 suites, 3 cottages
Double: $230–$1,010
Open May through October, Credit cards: all major
Restaurant: all meals
Handicap room

The Wedgewood Inn's brochure describes it as a romantic, fashionable, and sophisticated small inn meticulously restored to early nineteenth-century charm—and that truly sums it up. The inn is situated well back from Route 6A, the north shore route that travels along picturesque Cape towns with histories dating back to the days of merchant ships and fishing villages. Constructed in 1812 as the home of a maritime attorney, this was the first architect-designed home built in Yarmouth Port. Each of the guestrooms in the house and the beautifully restored barn with its hand-hewn beams is a delight, with outstanding attention to detail in the decor. There are handcrafted cherry-wood pencil-post beds, antique quilts, wide-board floors, wood-burning fireplaces, period wallpapers, and distinctive paintings. My favorite rooms were in the restored barn, particularly those upstairs off the balcony with their vaulted ceilings, old beams, and doors opening onto decks. The main dining room where breakfast is served has tables for two dressed with flowers and fine china, and bow-back Windsor chairs. The inn has air conditioning. *Directions:* From Boston take Route 3 south, over the Sagamore Bridge to Route 6. Take exit 7 to Willow Street and turn right. At the stop sign turn right onto Route 6A—the inn is on the right. If time permits, take Route 130 from Route 3 (just over the bridge) and then follow Route 6A along the beautiful north shore to the inn.

WEDGEWOOD INN
Innkeepers: Gerrie & Milt Graham
83 Main Street, Route 6A
Yarmouth Port, MA 02675
Tel: (598) 362-5157 or (508) 362-9178
Fax: (508) 362-5851
E-mail: info@wedgewood-inn.com
3 rooms, 6 suites, Double: $140–$205
Open all year
Credit cards: all major
Restaurant: none
Handicap room: none

New Hampshire
Places to Stay-Map 4

Bethlehem
Harts Location
Jackson Village
North Conway

16
302
16
91
93

Holderness
3

White River Junction

91
89

Henniker
Concord
Hopkinton
Francestown
Manchester
Hancock
Chesterfield

9
101
95
95
93
137
3

● Places to Stay
○ Points of Reference

a	b
c	d

Quadrants

Adair sits on top of a hill in a stunning, 200-acre country estate encompassing rock walls, ponds, and gardens, with lovely views of the White Mountains. Its main house, painted white, is a great example of the architecture of the 1920s and is furnished elegantly with period antiques or fine reproductions. The entrance hallway is large and the dining and living rooms flow from each side. The guestrooms, many with fireplaces, have queen or king beds and private bathrooms. The Kinsman is a large suite with a king sleigh bed, floor-to-ceiling windows, and a door leading to a private balcony. It also has a fireplace with comfortable reading chairs and the largest two-person whirlpool tub I've ever seen. The Waterford room offers a cherry-wood queen bed, a corner fireplace with sitting area, and a new bathroom with a two-person soaking tub. On the lower level you can relax in the Tap Room with its regulation pool table and in several comfortable sitting areas. In the afternoon when you return from the day's activities, tea is served with scrumptious cakes or cookies and, in season, dinner is available on Wednesday through Sunday in the lovely dining room. If you stay here you'll want to save some time for a stroll on the many trails surrounding the inn. *Directions*: Leave I-93 at exit 40 onto Route 302 east, turn sharp left at the Adair sign, and follow signs to the inn. From the east, take Route 302 west for about 3 miles past Bethlehem, and turn right at the sign to the inn.

ADAIR
Innkeepers: Judy & Bill Whitman
80 Guider Lane, Bethlehem, NH 03574
Tel: (603) 444-2600 or (888) 444-2600
Fax: (603) 444-4823
E-mail: adair@connriver.net
7 rooms, 2 suites, 1 2-bed/1-bath cottage
Double: $185–$195, Suite: $210–$245, Cottage: $335
Open all year, 1-week closures possible Apr. & Nov.
Credit cards: all major
Restaurant: dinner (Wed. through Sun. in season)
Handicap room: none
www.karenbrown.com/ne/adair.html

Originally a 1787 New Hampshire farm, Chesterfield Inn today offers 15 guest accommodations in a variety of rooms that boast fireplaces, balconies, and full bathrooms with whirlpool tubs. Guestrooms put privacy and comfort first: they are spacious and traditionally decorated, and have self-controlled heating and air conditioning, telephones, TVs, and refrigerators. I looked at a room with flowered wallpaper, two wing chairs, and a king bed on top of which was a cozy quilt for napping. There were views out onto the lawn and the gardens surrounding the inn. The dining room serves dinner six nights a week except in the foliage season and food preparation emphasizes fresh ingredients in unique flavor combinations. The seafood served at the inn comes from Boston, herbs from the garden, and other produce from local farms, all making for a delicious dinner. The parlor, dining room, and terrace are ideal settings for functions as intimate as a family gathering or as large as a wedding. This inn is located right off the major north-south interstate and is ideally situated for an extended stay in the area or a stopover when coming or going. *Directions:* Take I-91 to exit 3, following Route 9 east for 3 miles to the inn on the left.

CHESTERFIELD INN
Innkeepers: Judy & Phil Hueber
Route 9, P.O. Box 155
Chesterfield, NH 03443
Tel: (603) 256-3211 or (800) 365-5515
Fax: (603) 256 6131
E-mail: chstinn@sover.net
13 rooms, 2 suites
Double: $150–$275, Suite: $200–$225
Closed Christmas Day
Credit cards: all major
Restaurant: breakfast & dinner (Monday–Saturday)
Handicap room: none

The historic Inn at Crotched Mountain dates back 175 years and has lots of charm with warm paneling, big fireplaces, and comfortable furniture. From the inn the views look out to the swimming pool and tennis courts and then in the distance to the Piscatagoug Valley—one of those splendid vistas that vary as the light of the morning changes into brilliant sunshine and then late in the day as the shadows creep across the distant hills. I had a memorable dinner in the fully-licensed dining room, which included a delicious fish entree with local vegetables. Most of the cozy bedrooms have views over the distant mountain range, all have comfortable chairs or a loveseat for reading. The bedrooms are cozy. The inn is a great place to stay if you enjoy walking and in the winter months you can get your exercise with cross-country or downhill skiing. From this location you have access to many local antique and craft shops. If you are as fond of English cockers as I am, then you can be sure that your welcome will be a friendly one as the family has three cocker spaniels in residence: Winslow, Lucy and Frances. The Inn at Crotched Mountain is open seasonally, so be sure to note their comings and goings when you plan your trip in this part of New Hampshire. *Directions:* Take I-93 north to Route 101, driving west to Route 114 then north to Goffstown. Take Route 13 southwest to New Boston, Route 136 west to Francestown, then Route 47 north for 2½ miles. Turn left onto Mountain Road after 1 mile.

THE INN AT CROTCHED MOUNTAIN
Innkeepers: Rose & John Perry
534 Mountain Road
Francestown, NH 03043
Tel: (603) 588-6840, Fax: (603) 588-6623
E-mail: perry-inncm@conknet.com
13 rooms, Double: $80–$140
Closed April & November
Credit cards: none
Restaurant: breakfast
Handicap room

The Hancock Inn has been around since 1789, the first year of George Washington's presidency, and stands on a quarter-mile stretch of Hancock's Main Street where every house is listed in the National Register of Historic Places. Wide pine floorboards, paneling on the walls, cozy fireplaces, an old tavern pub, and an excellent restaurant ensure you of a comfortable and pleasurable stay. Without any doubt, the bedroom with the most history in this guide is the one in this inn with walls beautifully hand-painted by the renowned itinerant painter, inventor, and writer, Rufus Porter. There are fourteen other guestrooms, all with private baths and eight with fireplaces. Handmade quilts, cable TV, telephone, and air conditioning are *de rigueur*. The tavern is a great place to meet other guests, have a drink, and play a game of checkers. The inn's restaurant, which has been awarded many honors, presents hearty American fare with a large serving of New England, like cranberry pot roast, Nantucket seafood chowder, and roasted duckling with rosemary-mint brown sauce. In the area you can go antiquing, pick apples, go for a hike, or cut your own Christmas tree. *Directions:* From New York take I-91 to Brattleboro then Route 9 to Keene to Route 123. Turn right to the inn.

THE HANCOCK INN
Innkeepers: Linda, Joe & Chris Johnson
33 Main Street
Hancock, NH 03449
Tel: (603) 525-3318 or (800) 525-1789
Fax: (603) 525-9301
E-mail: innkeeper@hancockinn.com
15 rooms, Double: $140–$235
Open all year
Credit cards: all major
Restaurant: breakfast & dinner
Handicap room
www.karenbrown.com/ne/thehancockinn.html

The Notchland Inn gives you the chance to get away from it all and yet be within a few miles of lots of activities. Built in the 1860s, this granite mansion is located on 100 acres of the White Mountain National Forest, sitting atop a knoll at the base of one mountain and looking across at two others. The inn has the air of a wonderful old summer home, a feeling that permeates every room. There are seven rooms and five suites, each with a wood-burning fireplace. Carter is a large two-room suite with the fireplace in the bedroom, a queen bed made of cherry with an arched headboard, and handmade stained glass hanging in two windows. There are a sofa and a rocker in the sitting room and a two-person spa tub in the bathroom. Doors open to a large deck with great views. On the second floor of the former one-room schoolhouse is the Dixville Suite, another two-room suite where you can lie in the country-French queen bed and look across the sitting room to the fireplace or to the view from window. In the bath there's a large corner soaking tub. The main house living room is especially fine, designed by Gustav Stickley, a founder of the Arts and Craft movement, and has lovely furniture of that style. The inn serves a five-course dinner six days a week in a romantic dining room overlooking the gardens and the pond. *Directions:* Take I-93 north to exit 35 to Route 3 north for 10 miles to Route 302. Turn right on Route 302 for 17½ miles to the inn on the right.

THE NOTCHLAND INN
Innkeepers: Les Schoof & Ed Butler
Route 302
Hart's Location, NH 03812
Tel: (603) 374-6131 or (800) 866-6131
Fax: (603) 374-6168
E-mail: notchland@aol.com
7 rooms, 5 suites
Double: $235–$300
Open all year, Credit cards: all major
Restaurant: breakfast & dinner
Handicap room: none
www.karenbrown.com/ne/thenotchlandinn.html

Who hasn't heard of Golden Pond and who wouldn't be delighted to stay at this inn perched on Shepard Hill among ancient pines with a 65-mile panoramic view of Squam Lake and the surrounding mountains? Impressive and enchanting at the same time, with beamed ceilings, fireplaces, moldings, and large gracious rooms, the house will delight you with its architectural details. The bedrooms are elegant and well appointed. The Buckingham Room's old-world charm made it the master bedroom, with a king four-poster with canopy, striking black-and-ivory decor, and double French doors leading to a private deck from which there are views of the lake and the foothills. The Stratford Room, decorated with a wall-mounted bearskin, deer antlers, snowshoes and sled, is just plain fun. With Persian rugs on the hardwood floor, chintz-fabric walls in terra cotta and cream, and barn-board bookcases, this room provides an enchanting blend of the primitive and the cozy. During the warmer months you can also stay in a delightful cottage at the inn's private beach. Dining in the inn's elegant dining room with its acclaimed cuisine is another of the pleasures of staying here, while in the afternoon you can enjoy a formal English tea. Tennis, swimming, croquet, badminton, and shuffleboard are available within the 14 acres of the estate. *Directions:* Take I-93 to exit 24, go east on Route 3 for 4-7/10 miles, then turn right at the inn sign.

THE MANOR ON GOLDEN POND
Innkeepers: Mary Ellen & Brian Shields
Route 3, Box T
Holderness, NH 03245
Tel: (603) 968-3348 or (800) 545-2141
Fax: (603) 968-2116
E-mail: manorinn@lr.net
25 rooms (carriage house & cottages open seasonally)
Double: $210–$375
Open all year, Credit cards: all major
Restaurant: breakfast & dinner
Handicap room: none
www.karenbrown.com/ne/themanorongoldenpond.html

It would be difficult at The Inn at Thorn Hill to choose the most outstanding feature: the food in the dining room, the extensive and impressive wine list, the comfortable rooms, all with private bath, or the congeniality of the innkeepers—all are fabulous and make for a wonderful stay. Set up on a hill, the 1895 Stanford White building offers a variety of accommodations in 19 bedrooms, 3 suites, and 3 deluxe cottages. I stayed in the Mt. Madison on the second floor with its antique carved-wood queen bed and vanity, a blue velvet fainting couch, gas fireplace, and spa tub in the bathroom. The Carriage House, a short walk from the inn on the way to the pool, has six rooms, a deck for summer relaxation, and a year-round hot tub. Several of the rooms here have Jacuzzis and there is a living room providing a great place to relax with friends around the fireplace. The dinner I had was wonderful, from the crabmeat/avocado/sundried tomato appetizer to the duck breast with a pinot noir-mustard sauce and a grape and fennel agro dolce. I was too full for dessert, though the crème brulée served with crème anglaise and berry puree looked most tempting. Outdoor activities abound in the area, with easy access to major ski resorts and any number of sports. This inn is a great place for a restorative getaway or a romantic interlude. *Directions:* From Boston take I-95 north to the Spaulding Turnpike then Route 16 north to Jackson. Follow signs to the inn.

THE INN AT THORN HILL
Innkeepers: Ibby & Jim Cooper
Thorn Hill Road, P.O. Box A
Jackson Village, NH 03846
Tel: (603) 383-4242 or (800) 289-8990
Fax: (603) 383-8062
E-mail: thornhll@ncia.net
19 rooms, 3 suites, 3 deluxe cottages
Double: $190–$395*, *Includes dinner
Credit cards: all major
Restaurant: breakfast & dinner
Handicap room: none
www.karenbrown.com/ne/theinnatthornhill.html

Located away from the bustling commercial areas of North Conway, The Buttonwood Inn sits on a hill amidst 17 acres of fields and forest—yet it's just minutes to the ski areas and to town. This inn was originally an 1820s farmhouse and the owners have retained that country atmosphere with Shaker furniture, antiques, quilts, and period stenciling. There are ten simply but comfortably decorated bedrooms, each with private bath. My favorite was a room painted in a shade of cream that had a pencil-post four-poster queen bed, wonderful wide-board floors, scattered area rugs, a sofa, gas fireplace, spa tub for two, TV, and telephone. Breakfasts are special here and entrees are cooked to order. Guests have no trouble finding a good restaurant for dinner in North Conway or Jackson. When you're not out exploring the surrounding area, you can swim in the inn's pool, enjoy the award-winning gardens, and hike or cross-country ski right in the back yard. North Conway offers seven major ski resorts, more than 200 tax-free shops and outlets, over 50 restaurants, golf, tubing, kayaking, canoeing, fishing, ice-skating, snowshoeing, and sleigh rides. *Directions:* From Boston take I-95 to the Spaulding Turnpike to Route 16 north to North Conway. In the village turn right on Kearsarge Street for 1½ miles to the stop sign. Cross the intersection and drive up the hill to the inn.

THE BUTTONWOOD INN
Innkeepers: Claudia & Peter Needham
Mt. Surprise Road, P.O. Box 1817
North Conway, NH 03860
Tel: (603) 356-2625 or (800) 258-2625
Fax: (603) 356-3140
E-mail: innkeeper@buttonwoodinn.com
10 rooms, Double: $95–$225
Closed April
Credit cards: all major
Restaurant: none
Handicap room
www.karenbrown.com/ne/thebuttonwoodinn.html

154

Rhode Island - Places to Stay-Map 5

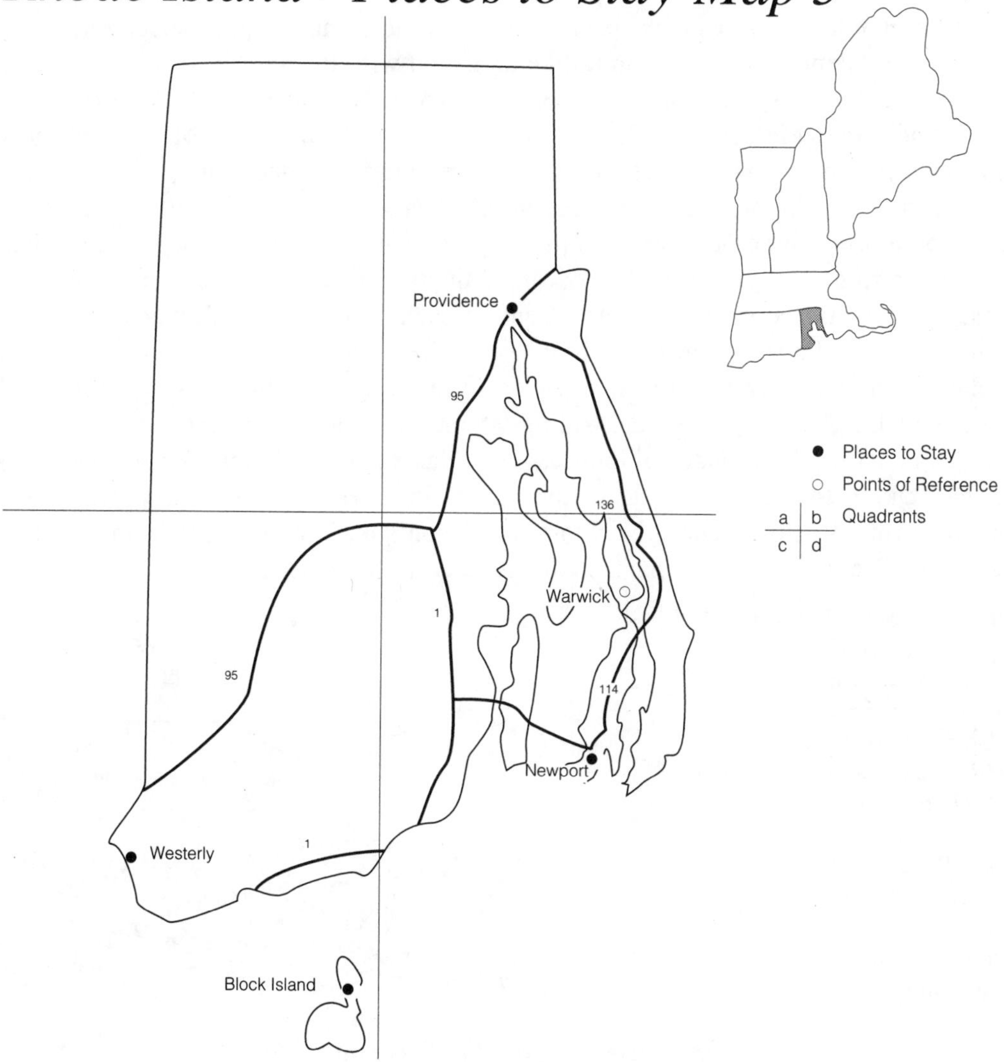

Providence

95

136

Warwick

1

95

114

Newport

Westerly

1

Block Island

- ● Places to Stay
- ○ Points of Reference

| a | b | Quadrants |
| c | d | |

Block Island, described by the Nature Conservancy as "one of the last 12 great places in the Western Hemisphere," can be reached by ferry or plane from Connecticut, Rhode Island, or Long Island. There is nothing like an island with its magical feeling of being a place apart—in this unspoiled spot you really feel you have stepped back in time. The 1661 Inn and Hotel Manisses, with sixty rooms in seven buildings, offers a range of delightful accommodations. Guestrooms are individually decorated, with various combinations of whirlpool tubs, decks, ocean views, and wood-burning fireplaces. Some rooms accommodate three or more persons, very convenient for families. There are wide porches for sitting and gazing at the ocean with its ever-changing activity and light. Breakfast (at the 1661 Inn) includes a hot entree each morning, and dinner, showcasing local seafood, is enjoyed at the Hotel Manisses, where you find fine dining in a casual atmosphere. On this island there is much or little to do—strolling along wide sandy beaches, bicycling, hiking, horseback riding, shopping, boating, fishing, bird watching, kayaking, or visiting historical lighthouses—or relaxing at the hotel with a good book. Guests can take a tour of the island in the inn's van. *Directions:* By ferry: from Point Judith (year round), Providence, Newport, and Montauk, NY. By air: from Newport, Westerly, and Providence or by charter. Contact the inn for schedules.

THE 1661 INN & HOTEL MANISSES
Innkeepers: Joan & Justin Abrams,
  and Rita & Steve Draper
P.O. Box 1, 1 Spring Street
Block Island, RI 02807
Tel: (401) 466-2421 or (800) 626-4773
Fax: (401) 466-3162
E-mail: biresorts@aol.com
60 rooms, Double: $50–$350
Open all year
Credit cards: all major
Restaurant: breakfast & dinner
Handicap room

Inns perched on a point of land with views of the sea, mountains, or a lake seem to be very special and the Castle Hill Inn & Resort is no exception. Its 40 acres at the west end of Newport's world-renowned Ocean Drive provide guests with the romance, the seclusion, and the beauty of an oceanside resort. This Victorian mansion has been elegantly restored, with guestrooms in the main building, the private Harbor Houses, and a Swiss-style chalet. There are also ten rustic beach cottages, which are open only in summer. The rooms have breathtaking views, king beds, fireplaces, and beautifully equipped bathrooms. In the main house bedrooms are decorated with Victorian furniture, while the other guestrooms are decorated in a more traditional style. All are comfortable and inviting. Castle Hill's dining room rises to match the extraordinary beauty of the inn's location and any meal here, including a decadent afternoon tea, is an experience not to miss. Newport is such a small, intimate town and the mansions are so extraordinarily large that a visit here garners a near-perfect ten. Don't miss the Cliff Walk—perfect for a picnic on a summer's day. *Directions:* From New York City take I-95 to Route 138 east. Take the first exit off the Newport Bridge and turn right at the second light. Turn right on Americas Cup then at the fifth light turn right on Thames to Wellington and then right on Ocean Drive for 3 miles. The inn is on the right.

CASTLE HILL INN & RESORT
General Manager: Paul O'Reilly
590 Ocean Drive
Newport, RI 02840
Tel: (401) 849-3800 or (888) 466-1355
Fax: (401) 849-3838
E-mail: info@castlehillinn.com
23 rooms, 2 suites, Double: $250–$550
Open all year
Credit cards: all major
Restaurant: all meals, Handicap room
www.karenbrown.com/ne/castlehill.html

Inns with great stories of past owners are not only special, but also make a stay memorable for travelers. For about 40 years the legendary artist Beatrice Turner lived a sheltered life in this fabulous Victorian manor house and in that time created a vast number of paintings of herself—over 100 of her artworks are on display in the inn. All the 16 rooms and suites have fireplaces, private baths, air conditioning, telephones, and cable TV. The unusual Tower Suite features a Victorian cupola tower and octagon cathedral ceiling, Queen Eastlake bed, fireplace, and bay window with its own seat for gazing out at the world below. There's morning coffee room service, a full gourmet breakfast, and afternoon Victorian tea. The inn is decorated with fine period antiques—a special piece is an original Tiffany lamp—and the fabrics used on the upholstered pieces are luxurious. Add to all the above warm hospitality, good company, genial innkeepers, and fine food, and you will enjoy a stay you'll long remember. The inn is perfectly located a five-minute walk from the beach on a quiet, tree-lined street, a half block from the Cliff Walk, Newport's renowned seaside walking trail in front of its even more legendary mansions. *Directions*: From New York City take I-95 north to exit 3 in Rhode Island for Route 138 east into Newport. From Boston take I-93 south to Route 24 south then Route 138 south. The inn is on the corner of Cliff and Seaview.

CLIFFSIDE INN
Innkeeper: Stephan Nicolas
2 Seaview Avenue
Newport, RI 02840
Tel: (401) 847-1811 or (800) 845-1811
Fax: (401) 848-5850
E-mail: cliff@wsii.com
8 rooms, 8 suites
Double: $225–$345, Suite: $315–$500
Open all year, Credit cards: all major
Restaurant: none
Handicap room: none
www.karenbrown.com/ne/cliffsideinn.html

Located on a winding country road in Seekonk, Massachusetts, yet just a ten-minute drive from Providence, the Jacob Hill Farm Bed and Breakfast Inn was built in 1722 and was once known as the Jacob Hill Hunt Club, which was patronized by the legendary Vanderbilts. Today this property has been transformed into an inn, with guestrooms providing all the comforts a traveler might expect. All the rooms are individually decorated and the private bathrooms have been updated, some with Jacuzzi tubs. A few of the rooms have fireplaces and many of the old wooden floors are covered with Oriental rugs. The owners have decorated one room with a scenic mural and have innovatively made use of canopies as decor over some of the antique beds. The Country Cottage, a separate building, offers an eat-in kitchen. There is air conditioning for the summer months if the usual breeze here on top of the hill isn't blowing. On the property you find a swimming pool and tennis court and there are plenty of places to sit, relax, and look out over the valley below. The owners take great pride in every detail of this inn that they have created and their breakfasts are no exception—there is a different hot entree every morning and with accompanying bacon or sausage, you'll have a great start to the day's activities. *Directions:* From Providence take I-195 east and leave at Massachusetts exit 1, turning left at the light (Route 114A). After about 1.7 miles turn right on Route 44, then after a 1 1/2 miles turn left on Jacob Street. The inn is on the left at the top of the hill.

HISTORIC JACOB HILL FARM B & B INN
Innkeepers: Eleanora & Bill Rezek
P.O. Box 41326
Providence, RI 02940
Tel: (508) 336-9165 or (888) 336-9165
Fax: (508) 336-0951
E-mail: Jacob-hill-farm@Juno.com
3 rooms, 2 suites, 1 cottage, Double: $120–$275
Open all year, Credit cards: all major
Restaurant: none, Handicap room: none
www.karenbrown.com/ne/jacobhillfarm.html

I have happy memories of visits as a child to this stretch of the Rhode Island coast. On the shore road, just a short distance from the magnificent beaches, sits The Villa, an inn of six guestrooms where you can enjoy the gardens and the pool as much as the inn's interiors. There is also a hot tub if you like to stare into the night from a steaming, refreshing cauldron. The inn's living room is comfortably furnished and there is an adjoining dining area where guests have breakfast (a full breakfast is served on weekends and a Continental one during the week). Two of the bedrooms are located in a separate building looking down into the gardens and the pool. I especially liked one with its own spa tub for two. The Villa is located in an area close to the quaint historic village of Watch Hill with its many shops and harbor activity. One of the remaining carousels in our country is found here and it provides a great opportunity to relive your childhood. Mystic Seaport and Newport are possible day excursions and the inn would be a good spot from which to take a trip to Block Island. Nearby beaches are great for walking as well as for swimming. *Directions*: Take I-95 to the Westerly area—ask the inn to fax or mail detailed directions, which, though somewhat complicated, are not hard to follow.

THE VILLA
Innkeepers: Angela Craig & Peter Gagnon
190 Shore Road
Westerly, RI 02891
Tel: (401) 596-1054 or (800) 722-9240
Fax: (401) 596-6268
E-mail: villa@riconnect.com
6 rooms, Double: $130–$255
Open all year
Credit cards: all major
Restaurant: none
Handicap room: none

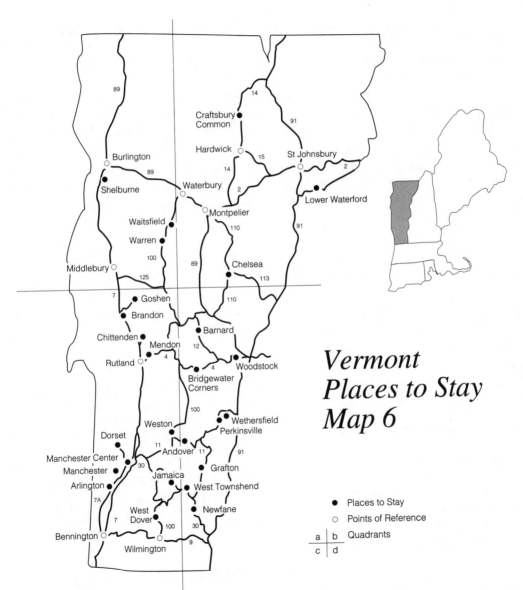

Craftsbury
Common ●

14

91

Hardwick ○   15   St Johnsbury ○   2

14   2

Burlington ○

89

Waterbury ○

Shelburne ●

Waitsfield ●   ○ Montpelier   Lower Waterford ●

Warren ●   110

100   91

Middlebury ○   89   Chelsea ●

125   113

7   ● Goshen

110

● Brandon

Chittenden ●   ● Barnard

Mendon

Rutland ○   4   4   ● Woodstock

Bridgewater
Corners

100

Weston ●   ● Wethersfield
Perkinsville ●

Dorset ●

11   Andover ●   11

Manchester Center ●   30   91

Manchester ●   Jamaica   ● Grafton

Arlington ●   ● West Townshend

7A

West   ● Newfane

Dover ●

7   100   30

Bennington ○   ○

Wilmington

9

*Vermont
Places to Stay
Map 6*

● Places to Stay
○ Points of Reference

| a | b | Quadrants |
| c | d | |

161

Built in 1820 as a stagecoach stop by Major Edward Simons, the historic Rowell's Inn sits right up front on a small country road and waits to greet you as a guest. Around the turn of the century the inn changed hands and the elegant tin ceilings, cherry and maple dining-room floors, central heating, and indoor plumbing were added. This is not a fancy inn, but rather one in which you will be very comfortable for a night's rest as you visit this portion of Vermont. Bedrooms have private bathrooms and are nicely furnished. The Miss Caitlin Room has a brass queen bed with canopy, blue flowered wallpaper, wonderful wide-plank floors, a wood-burning fireplace, and a bathroom with a tub and hand-held showerhead. The Miss Juliette Room has both a double and a twin bed. On the third floor the F. A. Rowell Suite has a double bed, a claw-foot tub, and a towel warmer (for me one of life's nicest amenities). The Major Simons Suite has a king bed and a ceiling fan. As one would expect, there's a dark, wonderfully atmospheric tavern room— it's easy to imagine the gatherings there almost 200 years ago. This room contains a most incredible wood-burning stove—I'd like to have brought it home. The inn's restaurant serves breakfast and a four-course dinner with a single entree. Note that there are no telephones or TVs in the rooms. *Directions:* On Route 11 connecting Route 7 and I-91. The inn is 7 miles west of Chester and 7 miles east of Londonderry.

ROWELL'S INN
Innkeeper: Louise Riehl-Haley
1834 Simonsville Road
Andover, VT 05143
Tel: (802) 875-3658 or (800) 728-0842
Fax: (802) 875-3680
E-mail: innkeep@rowellsinn.com
6 rooms, Double: $110–$165,
* $140–$195 with breakfast & dinner*
Credit cards: all major
Restaurant: breakfast & dinner
Handicap room: none

West Mountain Inn sits way up on a hill with glorious views down the long winding driveway to the valley below. There are 150 acres on which to roam, with wildflowers, a bird sanctuary, hiking trails, and the Battenkill River where you might want to try your fishing skills. Accommodation in the main house is in twelve bedrooms and three suites. The Booker T. Washington room has original pine paneling, your choice of either king or twin beds, and views of neighboring mountains and pastures. The Rockwell Kent suite has a native-pine cathedral ceiling in the king-sized bedroom and a spacious living room with fireplace. There are three townhouses at the historic mill, which may be taken with or without meals. Each of these has a living room with satellite TV, kitchen, master bedroom, and a cozy guestroom. The restaurant serves hearty country breakfasts and elegant six-course dinners seven days a week. Whether it's winter or summer or the peak time of foliage when all of New England comes ablaze, this inn is a great place to be. *Directions:* Leave Route 7 north at exit 3, turning left at the end of the ramp. Take the access road to end and turn right on Route 7A into Arlington. Drive 1 mile then turn left on Route 313 for 5/10 mile, go left on River Road, over the green bridge, and into the inn's driveway on the left.

WEST MOUNTAIN INN
Innkeepers: The Carlson Family
River Road
Arlington, VT 05250
Tel: (802) 375-6516, Fax: (802) 375-6553
E-mail: info@westmountaininn.com
12 rooms, 3 suites, 3 townhouses
Double: $155–$221*, Suite: $155–$269*,
  Townhouse: $155–$249*,
  *Includes breakfast & dinner
Open all year
Credit cards: all major
Restaurant: breakfast & dinner, Sunday brunch
Handicap room

Absolute perfection—your own farmhouse home in Vermont on 300 acres with country charm, urban sophistication, ingenious decoration, and every amenity in the world—at a price, but unique. In the evening guests come together for cocktails, wine and for lively conversation in the Barn Room, a large but warmly gracious room with fireplace and groupings of comfortable sofas and chairs. The dining room has vaulted ceilings with yet another blazing fire. There is no menu, but you will be dazzled by the chef's imaginative creations using the very freshest and finest ingredients. Meals leave your senses satiated and you ready to linger over a brandy in the pub. There are four guestrooms in the main house and eleven cottages connected by winding roads but otherwise serenely separate, each with its own style of decor and each in its own setting. I loved the Meadow Cottage, a Moroccan fantasy inside a Vermont clapboard structure—it's nothing short of a desert king's traveling palace. There's wonderful tile, a cozy sitting area in front of the fire, and a majestic bedchamber with hand-wrought bronze columns supporting a tented ceiling. The bathroom echoes this decor with its large tub, shower, and plush amenities. The inn also has a fitness room, a guest entertainment center, and everything else you might want. *Directions:* Take I-91 to I-89 to Route 107. Drive south on Route 12 to the town of Barnard, go past the post office and the inn is on the right.

TWIN FARMS
Managers: Beverley & Shaun Matthews
Barnard, VT 05031
Tel: (802) 234-9999 or (800) 894-6327
Fax: (802) 234-9990
4 rooms, 11 cottages
Double: $900–$1600, everything included
Open all year
Credit cards: all major
Restaurant: all meals, for resident guests only
Handicap room

Brandon, another of New England's small historic towns located on Route 7, was chartered in 1746 and sits in the valley between the Adirondacks and the Green Mountains. In 1909 Albert Farr built a summer cottage here in the Greek Revival style, with a five-arched façade that rivaled the finest homes in Brandon. New owners took over in 1991 and restored the somewhat neglected structure to its original splendor, not thinking at the time of creating an inn. In 1993, however, the Shanes decided to share their home, offering nine bedrooms each with private bath, and now visitors here feel as if they are guests in the era in which the house was originally built. There are two dining rooms, the casual tavern and the more formal West Garden Room, whose menu focuses on the creative use of Vermont produce and has won numerous awards for the inn. The inn's lovely setting and excellent reception facilities make it a popular choice for weddings. Brandon is situated near the major ski mountains and near Lakes Champlain and Dunmore, with rivers and streams creating great opportunities for fishing, swimming, and boating. Other attractions nearby include golfing and all the activities of the college town of Middlebury. Shelburne Museum is within an easy day's visit. *Directions:* From the north or south follow Route 7 to Brandon then take Route 73 east to the inn.

THE LILAC INN
Innkeeper: Michael Shane
53 Park Street
Brandon, VT 05733
Tel: (802) 247-5463 or (800) 221-0720
Fax: (802) 247-5499
E-mail: lilacinn@sover.net
9 rooms, Double: $125–$260
Open all year
Credit cards: all major
Restaurant: breakfast, dinner,
  Wednesday through Saturday
Handicap room: none

Think casual, think relaxed, think of a place where you can put your feet up, read a book, and be totally natural and without pretense. Think October Country Inn! In this quaint, ten-bedroom inn, a 19th-century farmhouse, you'll find sincere hospitality and delicious food. This is the kind of inn where they will put an extra bed in the room for that third person traveling with you. Some of the upstairs bedrooms are under the eaves but they're quite spacious enough for a good night's rest. Rooms have flowered wallpapers and a variety of brass, iron, and wooden headboards. Be sure to save some time to sit by the fire in the living room: a table behind the sofa had so many games on it, I couldn't figure out which I'd play first. While staying here I'd plan to spend some time in the kitchen, which has the look of a serious chef's domain. This inn is noted for its food and its reputation has spread far and wide. There's a swimming pool in the grounds, gardens for walking in, and plenty of diversions nearby—skiing, golf, cycling, summer theatre, and antiquing, to name just a few. One of the guests wrote in the inn's guest book, "I think I'll stay forever and send for my family." Maybe… *Directions:* From Woodstock drive 8 miles west on Route 4 to the junction with Route 100A. Continue on Route 4 for 200 yards, take the first right (opposite Long Trail Brewery), then right again to the inn.

OCTOBER COUNTRY INN
Innkeepers: Richard Sims & Patrick Runkel
Upper Road
P.O. Box 66
Bridgewater Corners, VT 05035
Tel: (802) 672-3412 or (800) 648-8421
Fax: (802) 672-3412
E-mail: oci@vermontel.net
10 rooms, Double: $129–$165
Closed April & first 3 weeks of November
Credit cards: all major
Restaurant: breakfast & dinner
Handicap room: none

Chelsea, a town with history from the early 19th century, is in the real Vermont that existed before the pace of our world demanded shopping centers, movie complexes, and everything convenient. You reach Chelsea down winding country roads past farms, dairies, streams, pristine schools, and white community churches. The historic Shire Inn, with six bedrooms and a two-bedroom cottage, helps you to rediscover the soul of our country. The Windsor is a large room on the second floor with a canopied queen bed, fireplace, wing chair, rocker, and both shower and tub. Four windows look out the front and the side of the building. The Bennington, a large second-floor room, has a king bed, fireplace, wing chair, rocker, and bathroom with stall shower. There are three smaller rooms on the second floor and a large room with fireplace on the first. The inn serves dinner and you can bet that the food will receive the same personal attention that's given to every detail by the attentive innkeepers. Before you leave be sure to take a photo of the beautiful winding staircase—it's New England at its finest. *Directions:* Leave I-89 at exit 2 (Sharon). Turn left, go 150 yards to the stop sign, turn right onto Route 14 for 7 miles, then go right on Route 110 for 13 miles to Chelsea. Leave I-91 at exit 14, go left on Route 113 and drive 23 miles to the end. Turn left and go 200 yards to the inn.

SHIRE INN
Innkeepers: Karen & Jay Keller
Main Street
Chelsea, VT 05038
Tel: (802) 685-3031 or (800) 441-6908
Fax: (802) 685-3871
E-mail: stay@shireinn.com
6 rooms, 2-bedroom cottage
Double: $115–$190,
  Cottage: $390 for 3 days, $550 per week
Closed Mar., Apr. & Nov., Credit cards: all major
Restaurant: breakfast & dinner
Handicap room: none
www.karenbrown.com/ne/shireinn.html

A long drive through the Green Mountain National Forest brings you to the Mountain Top Inn perched atop a plateau 2,000 feet above sea level, close to the Chittenden Reservoir, in a setting that promises total rest and relaxation. As I approached the inn after driving through the pristine wilderness, I stopped in my tracks as I gazed at views that are nothing short of spectacular. Inside, there's a dramatic fireplace in the living room, and above the stairs leading down to the dining room is a Tiffany bell-shaped chandelier original to the house. The inn has 35 bedrooms, all decorated with country charm, with twin or queen beds covered with colorful quilts. Most rooms have love seats, which in some cases open to accommodate additional guests. Views from all the rooms are spectacular. There is also a scattering of cottages and chalets, varying in size from one to four bedrooms, all having fireplaces or pot-bellied stoves and kitchens. Mountain Top's restaurant serves dinner every night in season—a good thing since the closest restaurant is not just down the block. Outdoor activities abound, with skiing, sleigh rides, skating, sledding, and building snowmen in winter; swimming, tennis, golf, canoeing, fishing, and horseback riding in summer. This is a perfect inn for children since there's so much to do and there's always plenty of company. *Directions:* Leave Route 7 at Rutland and drive northeast on Route 4 for 10 miles. Follow the state signs to the inn.

MOUNTAIN TOP INN & RESORT
Innkeepers: Maggie & Mike Gehan
Mountain Top Road, Chittenden, VT 05737
Tel: (802) 483-2311 or (800) 445-2100
Fax: (802) 483-6373
E-mail: info@mountaintopinn.com
35 rooms, 6 cottages & 6 chalets
Double: $196–$268, room only,
  $238–$310 with breakfast & dinner
Closed April & early November to late December
Credit cards: all major
Restaurant: breakfast & dinner (every night in season)
Handicap room

The inn's publicity material urges you to "Just think of it as a cruise ship in port for a few days," and the Tulip Tree is indeed a self-contained, secluded little world. Such is its tradition—it was originally the "getaway" home of William Barstow, one of Thomas Edison's collaborators, who came here with his family to get away from the bustle of urban life. The common areas are warm and friendly: my favorite is the den with its large windows and stone fireplace. The largest bedroom would be my first choice: it's 23 by 18 feet in size with five windows on one side, a fireplace, a dressing room with a large closet, air conditioning and a ceiling fan. The bathroom has a two-person Jacuzzi, a two-person shower, a two-sink vanity, and a fireplace. Room 4 was another of my favorites with its two green wingback chairs, hunter-green walls with cream trim, and a floral comforter in greens and pinks. These same colors are echoed in the floral wallpaper. Some of the bedrooms in this inn are located on the first floor for those who do not want to climb stairs. You can choose the options of bed and breakfast or bed, breakfast, and dinner. *Directions:* The inn is 10 miles northeast of Rutland. From Rutland take Route 7 north or Route 4 east and follow state signs to the inn.

TULIP TREE INN
Innkeepers: Rosemary & Ed McDowell
49 Chittenden Dam Road
Chittenden, VT 05737
Tel: (802) 483-6213 or (800) 707-0017
Fax: (802) 483-2623
E-mail: ttinn@sover.net
9 rooms, Double: $159–$419
Closed early April & early November
Credit cards: all major
Restaurant: breakfast & dinner
Handicap room: none
www.karenbrown.com/ne/tuliptreeinn.html

Craftsbury Common, way up in northern Vermont, is one of those absolutely perfect villages and The Inn on the Common is one of those places where you want to stay forever. Here the stars hang just above the white clapboard houses and the air is so pure that you wonder how much you can stand. The inn has sixteen guestrooms, each with private bath, located in three buildings, two across the street from each other and one a quarter of a mile up the road just off the common. Room 10 in the South Annex has a queen fishnet canopy bed and a couch in front of the fireplace stove. Room 7 is a two-bedroom suite with a queen bed, fireplace, and two comfortable chairs in one room and a second small bedroom with twin beds in the other. The inn's restaurant is well known for its cuisine and its wine cellar. The imaginative menu, featuring locally grown produce, changes each evening. On the property guests enjoy a swimming pool, tennis court, and croquet court. This is a perfect area to visit if winter sports appeal to you—but if not, just grab a cozy chair in front of a fireplace and settle in for a while. Be sure to save some time for just walking around town—this is a real delight. *Directions:* Take I-91 north to exit 21 onto Route 2 west to Route 15 west. In Hardwick take Route 14 north for 7 miles, then turn right to the inn. From I-91 south, take exit 26 onto Route 58 west to Route 14 south. Drive 12 miles to the sign for Craftsbury Common and go left to the inn.

THE INN ON THE COMMON
Innkeepers: Penny & Michael Schmitt
North Main Street
Craftsbury Common, VT 05827
Tel: (802) 586-9619 or (800) 521-2233
Fax: (802) 586-2249
E-mail: info@innonthecommon.com
14 rooms, 2 suites
Double: $250–$300
Open all year
Credit cards: all major
Restaurant: breakfast & dinner
Handicap room: none

There are two things in Vermont that are just about perfect: one is the charming town of Dorset—quintessential New England—and the second is the hospitality of Linda and Jim, the owners and innkeepers of this wonderful property, Barrows House. This is an historic inn of nine buildings scattered about on eleven acres. The inn has a swimming pool, tennis courts, lawn games, bicycles, cross-country ski equipment, and a sauna. Not only are the rooms complete with every amenity, but the front desk has a supply of "forgotten" items such as hair dryers. The Halstead Suite is the most remote accommodation, located up the hill in the woods. It has a small bedroom with a queen bed, handmade quilt, and braided rugs on the floor. In the sitting room there's a loveseat in front of the wood-burning fireplace, TV/VCR, small fridge, and a bar sink. There is a little greenhouse off the back and a small patio for summer relaxation. The Stable Suite #2 in the old hay loft has wide floorboards, window seats in the bedroom, bathroom, and sitting room, cathedral ceilings, a gas fireplace, old barn beams, a king canopy bed, and a TV/VCR in the sitting room. The restaurant serves breakfast and dinner seven days a week. By the way, this is a great family inn: there were lots of kids everywhere when I visited. *Directions:* From either the north or south take Route 7 to Route 30 to Dorset—the inn is just outside the village.

BARROWS HOUSE
Innkeepers: Linda & Jim McGinnis
Route 30
Dorset, VT 05251-0098
Tel: (802) 867-4455 or (800) 639-1620
Fax: (802) 867-0132
E-mail: barhouse@vermontel.com
10 rooms, 7 suites, 3 cottages
Double: $140–$275, room only,
  $195–$275 with breakfast & dinner
Open all year, Credit cards: all major
Restaurant: breakfast & dinner, Handicap room
www.karenbrown.com/ne/barrowshouse.html

Located in what some say is the most charming village in America, the Cornucopia of Dorset, a bed and breakfast inn, is just a minute's walk from Dorset's village green. It fits in beautifully with the white clapboard homes of this community and its flowerboxes and bountiful baskets of impatiens add outside charm and color, hanging just on the other side of the front door. The inn is lovingly decorated with furnishings that make you want to settle in with a good book in front of the fireplace and an afternoon cup of tea—all the more enjoyable in the brisk air of the fall after you have walked about the village and poked in its few shops. The air-conditioned guestrooms are traditionally furnished, as you would expect in a restored 1880 Colonial. Four of these are in the main house and three of these have corner fireplaces. The beds are four-posters or canopied and have wool mattress covers, down pillows, and fluffy down comforters. There is also a cottage with loft bedroom and skylight, living room with cathedral ceiling and fireplace, fully equipped eat-in kitchen, large bath, and private deck. The inn serves delicious, candlelit breakfasts with freshly squeezed orange juice and gourmet entrees. Sterling silver, linens, and fresh flower arrangements add to the attractive ambiance of the dining room. *Directions:* The inn is located 6 miles north of Manchester on route 30 on the right as you enter the village of Dorset.

CORNUCOPIA OF DORSET
Innkeepers: Trish & John Reddoch
3228 Route 30, P.O. Box 307
Dorset, VT 05251
Tel: (802) 867-5751 or (800) 566-5751
Fax: (802) 867-5753
E-mail: innkeepers@cornucopiaofdorset.com
4 rooms, 1 cottage
Double: $130–$180, Cottage: $225–$270
Open all year, Credit cards: all major
Restaurant: none
Handicap room: none
www.karenbrown.com/ne/cornucopiaofdorset.html

Blueberry Hill invites you into their special, tranquil world in the Green Mountain National Forest, a world of quiet, fresh air, lovely food, and luxurious accommodations. In the main house, built in 1813, there are four bedrooms, two with double beds and two with twins; the Greenhouse has three rooms, each with a double bed and twin beds in a loft; and there are four Pondside rooms, each with a double bed. There is a cottage decorated with Colonial furnishings—primarily antiques and antique quilts—with a double room and two twins (perfect for families). The inn is a recreation destination, with skiing being the greatest attraction. Just a few minutes away is Lake Dunmore where you can swim and windsurf and boat. However, I could just as easily settle in and be perfectly content with nothing to do but read, relax, and take a walk into this pristine world. The inn has great trekking and trail guides for its guests. The cooking is gourmet here and meals are a real treat, with flowers from the inn's gardens decorating the plates of food as they come to your table. What a great visual feast this makes the dining experience. For 20 years the inn has been baking cookies and putting them in the cookie jar for guests and non-guests alike. Now cookies are available by mail to those who wish to order a memory of a time spent at Blueberry Hill. *Directions:* Off Route 73 east of Brandon, follow Forest Road. Off Route 125, 1 mile east of Ripton, follow Forest Road for 6 miles to the inn.

BLUEBERRY HILL
Innkeepers: Shari Brown & Tony Clark
Goshen, VT 05733
Tel: (802) 247-6735 or (800) 448-0707
Fax: (802) 247-3983
E-mail: info@blueberryhillinn.com
11 rooms, 1 cottage
Double: $120–$150 with dinner
Open all year
Credit cards: all major
Restaurant: breakfast & dinner
Handicap room

The Old Tavern at Grafton makes one of those architectural statements that you never forget—its façade is both wide and tall and it has an appealing porch that just beckons you to sit and relax. The main tavern and two cottages house fifty-one guestrooms and there are also seven guesthouses, most with full kitchens, which can each accommodate from eight to fourteen people. The Old Tavern prides itself on not having phones or TVs in the rooms so that guests can truly relax during their visit. I saw several of the rooms, which have flowered wallpapers and private baths with all the amenities, and are traditionally decorated in a comfortable style. The dining room is both attractive and traditional in its decor, with a lovely sideboard and tables set for two, four, or six. Your room rate includes a full country breakfast and afternoon tea. What's especially charming about this inn is its tavern pub, a short walk down the hall from the main building. Its two stories exude New England charm with old barn-board walls, hand-hewn timbered beams, and lots of cozy seating in front of the large wood-burning fireplace. The Old Tavern has its own stables so you can make arrangements to bring your horse—you could both have a great vacation in this New England town! The inn offers discounts to senior citizens and repeat guests. *Directions:* Take exit 5 off I-91—Grafton is located at the intersection of Routes 35 and 121.

THE OLD TAVERN
Innkeeper: Kevin O'Donnell
Main Street, P.O. Box 9
Grafton, VT 05146
Tel: (802) 843-2231 or (800) 843-1801
Fax: (802) 843-2245
E-mail: tavern@sover.net
51 rooms, 7 guesthouses
Double: $175–$260, Guesthouse: $620–$890
Open all year
Credit cards: all major
Restaurant: all meals
Handicap room

Three Mountain Inn has all you'll want for as long a time as you can be a guest. This romantic 1790s country inn on the main street of the little town of Jamaica, just under the shadow of the Green Mountains, is ideally located for access to skiing, but great for foliage, not far from shopping, and perfect for wandering. The living room with its large fireplace is warm and welcoming and the dining rooms are simply but tastefully furnished—what's complex is the tasty food that comes from the kitchen. The traditionally furnished bedrooms all have private baths and telephones. I stayed in Jamaica, a suite whose living room had a gas fireplace, a sofa and two wing chairs for reading, and Colonial-print wallpaper. The bedroom, painted pale, creamy yellow, had tables with good reading lights on either side of the four-poster queen bed. The Arlington, just down the hall, was furnished with a queen bed, an armoire, a sofa and a wing chair and had pale-cream-painted walls. Even though this is a sleepy mountain town, I'd probably choose one of the rooms at the back of the inn in order to be sure of a night's rest that is as refreshing as the style and welcome of the innkeepers. Oates & Bredfeldt, are in their 20th year of giving seminars to prospective innkeepers. *Directions:* From Brattleboro take I-91 to exit 2 and go north on Route 30. From Manchester take Route 30 south.

THREE MOUNTAIN INN
Innkeepers: Stacey & David Hiler,
 and Bill Oates & Heide Bredfeldt
Route 30, P.O. Box 180
Jamaica, VT 05343
Tel: (802) 874-4140 or (800) 532-9399
Fax: (802) 874-4745
E-mail: threemtn@sover.net
14 rooms, 1 cottage
Double: $115–$295, Cottage: $250–$295
Open all year, Credit cards: all major
Restaurant: breakfast & dinner
Handicap room: none
www.karenbrown.com/ne/threemountaininn.html

Afternoon tea was being served as I arrived at Rabbit Hill Inn—just what I had been thinking I would like. This was just one example of the way the innkeepers and staff here seem to anticipate your every need—they have honed the art of personal service to absolute perfection, with many thoughtful touches like transforming your bedroom with candlelight and soft music when you return to it after dinner. There are twenty-one rooms and suites with private bathrooms in two historic buildings—most have fireplaces and some have whirlpools tubs, but all are individual and special. I stayed on the second floor of the main building in the Canopy Chamber, a corner room with views of the White Mountains and the inn's gardens. The queen bed was waiting to share with me a perfect night's rest, the gas fireplace had a chaise longue in front of it with pillows to make me comfortable, and on the bed was a note from the staff asking if there was anything else I might want. The room also had a desk, a Boston rocker, and access to a lovely porch facing the mountains. The inn's dining room serves delectable, award-winning, five-course dinners. Rabbit Hill's 15 acres provide you with lawn games, a swimming pond, trails for hiking and skiing, fishing, and canoeing. *Directions*: From I-91 north or south, take exit 19 to I-93 south. Leave at exit 1, turning right onto Route 18 south for 7 miles to the inn. From I-93 north, take exit 44, turning left onto Route 18 north. Drive 2 miles to the inn.

RABBIT HILL INN
Innkeepers: Leslie & Brian Mulcahy
Route 18
Lower Waterford, VT 05848
Tel: (802) 748-5168 or (800) 762-8669
Fax: (802) 748-8342
E-mail: info@rabbithillinn.com
21 rooms, Double: $275–$380*, *Includes dinner
Closed early April & early November
Credit cards: all major
Restaurant: breakfast & dinner, Handicap room
www.karenbrown.com/ne/rabbithillinn.html

Perched on a hill with sweeping views of the valley below and the Green Mountains, The Inn at Ormsby Hill is a restored 1764 manor house listed on the Register of Historic Places. In this inn attention to detail is everywhere, in the decor of the common rooms and the bedrooms, and in the dining room where Chris is the master of her trade. Simply scrumptious breakfasts are served in the attractively decorated conservatory with its views out to the surrounding mountains. The living room made me feel completely at home—I could either curl up by the fire or simply relax in the luxurious surroundings. The ten guestrooms have canopied beds, fireplaces, spa tubs for two and, if you are visiting in the summer, air conditioning. All the rooms are great, but one of my favorites is wallpapered with a red-and-white print, has a gas fireplace with a small hooked rug in front, two comfortable chairs with a great reading light, a canopied bed, and a spa tub for two in the bathroom from which you can see the fireplace. There's a porch out back with old wicker furniture and a painted board floor, perfect for a second cup of breakfast coffee and a peaceful reverie. Innkeepers Chris and Ted are pros and I am sure that staying with them in the Manchester area will make for memories that will bring you back often. *Directions:* In Manchester Center, at the junction of Routes11, 30 and 7A, take historic Route 7A south. The inn is approximately 3 miles along on the left.

THE INN AT ORMSBY HILL
Innkeepers: Chris & Ted Sprague
1842 Main Street
Manchester Center, VT 05255
Tel: (802) 362-1163 or (800) 670-2841
Fax: (802) 362-5176
E-mail: stay@ornsbyhill.com
10 rooms, Double: $175–$370
Open all year
Credit cards: MC, VS
Restaurant: none
Handicap room

Not many historic structures have been operating since 1811, but this one has and its imposing architecture demands your attention as you drive through the beautiful town of Manchester. Within the walls of the original building and the adjacent cottage are fourteen guestrooms, the most romantic with fireplaces and one with a private balcony. I loved the cottage room that takes up the entire second floor and has a cathedral ceiling: from the bed you can see the fireplace and there's a comfortable pair of leather chairs for sitting and reading. The suite on the first floor of the main building and two rooms on the second floor have fireplaces, one has a king four-poster and the other two have queen canopy beds. The common rooms have wood-burning fireplaces and are furnished with English and American antiques, prints, and Oriental rugs. There's an inviting little pub with bar stools snuggled up to the highly polished dark-wood bar and a group of tables by the windows. One of the innkeepers has a passion for single-malt Scotch whisky and there's a collection of them that will far exceed your ability to taste. Scottish ale is also on tap. This property is deceiving in that it sits right on the main street but has 7 acres of land with a pond and gardens. From anywhere out back the views to the picturesque Green Mountains are yours to enjoy. *Directions*: In Manchester Center, at the junction of Routes 11, 30, and 7A, take Route 7A south. The inn is about 1 mile along on the left.

1811 HOUSE
Innkeepers: Marnie & Bruce Duff, Cathy & Jorge Veleta
Route 7A, P.O. Box 39
Manchester, VT 05254-0039
Tel: (802) 362-1811 or (800) 432-1811
Fax: (802) 362-2443
E-mail: stay1811@vermontel.net
14 rooms, Double: $120–$230
Closed Christmas & the week before Christmas
Credit cards: all major
Restaurant: none, but fully licensed British pub
Handicap room: none
www.karenbrown.com/ne/1811house.html

The Red Clover Inn is a retreat away from the cares of the world and we're glad that the original owner sought such a perfect spot for building in the 1840s. This inn truly feels like a private home—there is no sense that there are 14 guestrooms and that other guests must be somewhere. The beamed-ceilinged living room is most inviting with its fireside sofas and wonderful leather wingbacks. Guestrooms, all with private bathrooms, king or queen beds, and lovely mountain views, are in two buildings—seven in the main building and seven newer rooms in the carriage house. The three newest rooms are especially deluxe and extremely spacious, with king beds, whirlpool tubs from which you can see the gas fireplace, warm cherry-wood furniture, and beamed ceilings. Most of the inn's rooms have TVs and some have VCRs. A four-course dinner is included in the tariff, with a menu sumptuous in content and presentation. The inn is conveniently located near the major ski areas of central Vermont. There's a swimming pool for guests visiting in the summer, when hiking and horseback riding are also popular, while cross-country skiing is the sport of choice in the winter. Less strenuous activities include antiquing and attending concerts and plays. *Directions:* 5 miles west of Killington, turn left from Route 4 onto Woodward Road and drive ½ mile to the inn on the left. 5 miles east of Rutland, turn right from Route 4 onto Woodward Road and drive half a mile to the inn on the left.

RED CLOVER INN
Innkeepers: Sue & Harris Zuckerman
7 Woodward Road, Mendon, VT 05701
Tel: (802) 775-2290 or (800) 752-0571
Fax: (802) 773-0594
E-mail: redclovr@vermontel.net
11 rooms, 3 suites
Double: $200–$450*, *Includes dinner
Closed Easter Sunday to Memorial Day weekend
Credit cards: MC, VS
Restaurant: breakfast, dinner (Mon. through Sat.)
Handicap room: none
www.karenbrown.com/ne/redcloverinn.html

Newfane is a "must-visit," beautiful New England town and has been one of my favorites for 40 years or so. The historic green and all the houses that surround the county courthouse stand as they have since the 1840s and behind the courthouse you find the Four Columns Inn. The inn is a popular base for sightseeing in this area, and if you'd like to visit during foliage time (generally the first half of October), you'll need to make reservations as much as a year ahead. There are 15 guestrooms with gas fireplaces, private baths, telephones, modems, and fax available—the TV is in the common room. My personal favorite was room 12, with its king pencil-post cherry-wood bed and a fireplace open on one side to the bedroom and on the other to the bathroom. There's an attractive sitting area with two comfortable chairs, a painted armoire, and views of woods. The inn's restaurant produces impeccable, creative cuisine blending New American, Asian, and French traditions into taste sensations (once again, reservations are needed well in advance, even for houseguests). Presentations are so spectacular that it's hard to decide whether dinner looks better or tastes better. *Directions:* Leave I-91 at exit 2 in Vermont and turn left onto Western Ave for half a mile then turn left onto Cedar Street. At the stop sign turn left onto Route 30 north for 11 miles. The inn is on Newfane Green behind the county courthouse.

FOUR COLUMNS INN
Innkeepers: Pam & Gorty Baldwin
P.O. Box 278
Newfane, VT 05345
Tel: (802) 365-7713 or (800) 787-6633
Fax: (802) 365-0022
E-mail: innkeeper@fourcolumnsinn.com
9 rooms, 6 suites, Double: $135–$340
Closed December 24 & 25
Credit cards: all major
Restaurant: dinner
Handicap room: none

When I arrived in the small foyer of this 18th-century country inn, I was taken through the dining room to the living room, which was an extension of the same space. Candles had been lit in the dusk of the afternoon and lamps were turned low for an ambiance conducive for good conversation and relaxation. It's a memory of welcoming friendship I'll have for a long time. The dining room has a Steinway grand piano and chandeliers with real candles, which create a magic for those fortunate enough to be dining there. Guests also enjoy a parlor with antique furniture, a taproom where you can have a drink and play an 18th-century board game, and a game room with a tournament-size pool table, exercise equipment, and a Finnish sauna. Of course, if all that seems like too much, you can just sit on the front porch and watch the deer graze on the lawn. I'd probably sample all the above and then take the resident cat to my room for an afternoon nap. The 12 guestrooms have settings inspired by the grandest love stories of all time. Try the Regal Lodge with its king bed, rose-arch slipper tub, and Victorian parlor with private balcony. The Manderley has a lace-draped queen bed and its own sitting room decorated with romantic memorabilia. *Directions:* From I-91 north, take exit 7 onto Route 11 west to Route 106 north. The inn is 5 miles along on the left. From I-91 south, take exit 8 onto Route 131 west to Route 106 south. The inn is 3 miles along on the right.

THE INN AT WEATHERSFIELD
Innkeepers: Mary & Terry Carter
Route 106, P.O. Box 165
Perkinsville, VT 05151
Tel: (802) 263-9217 or (800) 477-4828
Fax: (802) 263-9219
11 rooms, 1 suite
Double: $150–$250
Open all year
Credit cards: all major
Restaurant: dinner (closed 2 days midweek off season)
Handicap room: none

It would be hard to imagine a more spectacular setting than that of The Inn at Shelburne Farms, which sits in a 1400-acre estate overlooking Lake Champlain and the Adirondack Mountains. The grounds are a creation of Frederick Law Olmsted, the architect who designed New York's Central Park. The estate is owned by a nonprofit organization devoted to "preserving, maintaining, and adapting its historic buildings and landscape for teaching and demonstrating the stewardship of natural and agricultural resources." The dramatic, 60-room Queen Anne mansion has 24 guestrooms, 17 with private baths, which are individual in their decor and vary dramatically in price and comfort. The most popular rooms are on the second floor, facing the lake and decorated with fine antiques. Of those, the W. Seward Webb bedroom has William Morris wallpaper and a massive double bed, while the handsome Empire Room has furnishings, drapes, and wall coverings of the Empire period. Tucked under the eaves of the third floor overlooking the garden are the least expensive rooms. Apart from touring Shelburne Farms itself, while you are in the area you must visit the Shelburne Museum with its collections of home crafts, folk art, fine arts and furnishings, the restored *Ticonderoga* steamship, and other exhibits from 300 years of life in America. *Directions:* Leave I-89 at Vermont exit 13 onto Route 7 south for 5 miles as far as the light in the center of Shelburne. Turn right onto Harbor Road to the first stop sign and go left into Shelburne Farms.

THE INN AT SHELBURNE FARMS
Manager: Karen Polihronakis
1611 Harbor Road
Shelburne, VT 05482
Tel: (802) 985-8498, Fax: (802) 985-8123
24 rooms, 17 with private bathrooms
Double: $95–$360*, *Breakfast not included
Open mid-May to mid-October
Credit cards: all major
Restaurant: breakfast & dinner
Handicap room: none

The Inn at the Round Barn Farm, sitting in 245 lovely acres of mountains, meadows, and ponds, promises romance, relaxation, and an escape from reality. On the day of my visit the first welcoming touch I encountered was a tureen of hot soup for returning skiers in the small but cozy library. The dining room, where you savor Anne Marie's wonderful breakfasts, has windows on both sides looking out to the surrounding hills and tables set in various sizes. The guestrooms are all very different from one another in their decor but all have private bathrooms, original pine floors, rich wallpapers, and plush terry robes. I stayed in the Abbott Room, a suite with a king four-poster with feather bed, a TV hidden in an armoire, a living room with a gas fireplace, an oversized two-person corner whirlpool tub, and separate bathroom steam shower and two-person vanity. Hand-hewn beams and plenty of windows complete the scene. An unusual amenity here is the 60-foot lap pool, which extends into a greenhouse filled with flowering plants. The inn has its own groomed, marked cross-country ski center and downhill skiing is just minutes away. The inn's Round Barn hosts weddings, conferences, concerts, and art exhibits. *Directions:* Take I-89 south to exit 10, then Route 100 south for 14 miles. (From I-89 north take exit 9 onto Route 100 north for 14 miles.) Turn onto Bridge Street, drive through the covered bridge, and bear right at the fork. The inn is 1 mile up on the left.

THE INN AT THE ROUND BARN FARM
Innkeeper: Anne Marie DeFreest
1661 East Warren Road
Waitsfield, VT 05673
Tel: (802) 496-2276, Fax: (802) 496-8832
E-mail: roundbarn@madriver.com
11 rooms, 1 suite, Double: $135–$275
Closed April & last half of November
Credit cards: all major
Restaurant: none
Handicap room: none
www.karenbrown.com/ne/theinnatroundbarnfarm.html

Throw away the books on decorating—start thinking outside the box and book fast at The Pitcher Inn in one of its fabulously decorated and themed rooms, whether it's The School Room, The Trout Room, The Lodge, The Hayloft, or The Ski Room. I suppose that the most spectacular has to be The Lodge with its massive four-poster bed with eagles sitting on top of the headboard and Egyptian, Greek, and Masonic-lodge influences. Its starry ceiling overhead with the constellations in place for Christmastime is just plain wonderful. Add a bathroom with marble slab walls, a steam room, a deep soaking Jacuzzi, and you are in heaven. The Ski Room uses relics from ski areas—old bamboo poles, skis, ticket windows, a bedspread made from ski jackets. Your entrance to the room is a stone walkway set into the carpet. The inn's common rooms have massive furniture into which you just sink and the downstairs lounge with its stone-walled atmosphere is our kind of place. The dining room serves magnificent food in a bright and elegant room whose tables are set with crisp white linens and sparkling silver and glasses. The simple windsor chairs make for a refined elegance. *Directions:* I-89, I-91, I-93, and I-95 will all bring you to the vicinity of the inn. From I-89 north take Route 100 south to Warren where you find The Pitcher Inn on Main Street in the center of the village.

THE PITCHER INN
Managers: Heather & John Carino
275 Main Street
P.O. Box 347
Warren, VT 05674
Tel: (802) 496-6350 or (888) 867-4824
Fax: (802) 496-6354
E-mail: pitcher@madriver.com
9 rooms, 2 suites, Double: $300–$550
Open all year
Credit cards: all major
Restaurant: breakfast & dinner
Handicap room

The Deerhill Inn and Restaurant sits perched high on a hill with views out to the ski areas of Haystack and Mount Snow. The downstairs living room is shared by non-resident guests coming for dinner but there is an upstairs living room that's reserved for inn guests. Decorating here is done with flair, incorporating lots of flowers and vines, and in fact Waverly Fabrics chose one of Deerhill's bedrooms as the room of the year in 1996. The inn has 15 guestrooms, a full-service bar, and a swimming pool. All bedrooms, four with king beds, have private baths, some have fireplaces, and some have superb views of the mountains. Room 5 is a suite with two rooms, with a king bed in the bedroom and a convertible sofa in the living room, which also has a TV and lovely mountain views. Double bedrooms are cozy and quaint, some decorated in blue and pink, some in green and yellow, others in pastels. The room referred to as "L2" (because it is one of the inn's two rooms with a loft), has a queen canopied bed with mosquito netting and is decorated with an Oriental theme. The restaurant presents imaginative country cuisine with an emphasis on seafood in a charming dining room with a fireplace, hand-painted murals, and spectacular views. You can stay here with either bed and breakfast only or bed, breakfast, and dinner. *Directions:* From I-91 take exit 2 to Route 9 west, driving 20 miles to Route 100 where you go north. Drive 6 miles to Valley View Road and go up the hill for 200 yards.

DEERHILL INN
Innkeepers: Linda & Michael Anelli
Valley View Road, P.O. Box 136
West Dover, VT 05356
Tel: (802) 464-3100 or (800) 993-3379
Fax: (802) 464-5474
E-mail: deerhill@sover.net
15 rooms & suites, Double: $165–$285
Open all year, Credit cards: all major
Restaurant: breakfast & dinner
Handicap room: none
www.karenbrown.com/ne/deerhillinn.html

The Inn at Sawmill Farm is imbued with old New England style and decor. You feel the warmth of this property as you climb the stairs to the reception area and the adjoining common room with its charming timbered ceilings, barn-board walls, and that ever-present New England fireplace. The bedrooms are swathed in floral fabrics and you're likely to find that the decor in your room is coordinated with a single pattern and color. Rooms are large and have all the amenities that you expect in a first-class inn. There's a world-class restaurant on the premises with a 34,000-bottle wine cellar. Dinners consist of five courses and the menu I saw was very sophisticated—sea bass, salmon, and lobster headed up the seafood, while the meats encompassed chicken, pork, duck, rabbit, veal, and venison—all prepared in very individual styles. With a great selection of cold and warm appetizers, dinner at this inn is a real pleasure. Breakfast time is no less grand, with a hot entree to give you a good start to the day's activities. Be sure to spend some time in the old tavern in the barn where the real charm of this New England inn is everywhere around you. The inn is located in the heart of Southern Vermont with more activities you could dream of, every sport imaginable, and with more antique shops than you can visit. *Directions:* Leave I-91 at Vermont exit 2. Take Route 9 west to Route 100 north approximately 6 miles to the village of West Dover—the inn is on the left after the village church.

THE INN AT SAWMILL FARM
Innkeeper: Brill Williams
Route 100 & Crosstown Road, P.O. Box 367
West Dover, VT 05356
Tel: (802) 464-8131 or (800) 493-1133
Fax: (802) 464-1130
E-mail: sawmill@sover.net
20 rooms, Double: $350–$570*, *Includes dinner
Closed April to May 27, Credit cards: all major
Restaurant: dinner
Handicap room
www.karenbrown.com/ne/theinnatsawmill.html

The Windham Hill Inn sits at the end of a country road on a rise with views all around. When I visited, I walked up the sidewalk and the full moon was just coming over the mountain in the distance. Inside the inn, there are lovingly decorated living rooms to make you feel instantly as if you've just returned to see an old friend. Fireplaces and comfortable chairs beckon and windows give magnificent views of ancient apple trees, gardens, and lawns. There are 21 guestrooms, most with fireplaces, several with large soaking tubs. I stayed in the White Barn in a first-floor room with a pot-bellied stove sitting in the corner, two luxuriously overstuffed chairs, and a sliding door to its own private deck. The bed was king-size, and the bath had a two-person whirlpool tub and a shower with two showerheads—a wonderful extravagance that made me linger just a few moments longer. The inn has an excellent dining room and the chef prepared a memorable dinner while I was there—the dessert of pear and apple with ice cream and a swirl of crisp cookie was as spectacularly presented as it was delicious. The innkeepers here are caring and want to be sure that your every moment will create a memory. The inn has an excellent conference/event center. *Directions:* Take I-91 north to Brattleboro, exit 2, to Route 30 and drive 21½ miles northwest to West Townshend. Turn right onto Windham Hill Road, drive 1-3/10 miles, and follow the sign to the inn.

WINDHAM HILL INN
Innkeepers: Pat & Grigs Markham
311 Lawrence Drive
West Townshend, VT 05359
Tel: (802) 874-4080 or (800) 944-4080
Fax: (802) 874-4702
E-mail: windham@sover.net
21 rooms, Double: $200–$325
Closed week before December 27
Credit cards: all major
Restaurant: dinner by reservation
Handicap room: none
www.karenbrown.com/ne/windhamhillinn.html

This National Historic Register inn has thirteen rooms in three buildings—the Markham House dating to 1848, the Coleman House (1830), and a charming country barn—all nestled on 6 acres of woods, lawn, and gardens on the banks of the West River. Within walking distance you find the village green, the famous Vermont Country Store, art galleries, the Weston Playhouse, museums, antique shops, and more. Weston (population 627) is another of those quaint New England towns situated along Route 100, one of the area's most scenic drives. The inn's common rooms are welcoming and comfortably furnished and there's a pub that just waits for your presence. The dining room offers dinners that will tantalize all your senses. I was able to see two guestrooms: the Waite had a king cherry-wood bed, a pot-bellied gas stove, a TV, a whirlpool bath from which you could peek into the bedroom, and a steam shower. Flowered wallpaper completed the decor. In the Parkhurst there was also a king bed, wingback chairs in front of the fireplace, TV, and a whirlpool bath. There are two suites in the carriage house. Not all the rooms have fireplaces, TV, or whirlpool tubs so if these are important to you, be sure to specify what you want when you make your reservation. *Directions:* Take I-91 north to Route 103 west through Chester to Londonderry. Turn right on Route 100 to Weston and to the inn on the left.

THE INN AT WESTON
Innkeepers: Lauren & Steve Bryant
Route 100
Weston, VT 05161
Tel: (802) 824-6789, Fax: (802) 824-3073
E-mail: inweston@sover.net
11 rooms, 2 suites, Double: $185–$325
Open all year
Credit cards: all major
Restaurant: breakfast & dinner
Handicap room: none

Woodstock, Vermont is one of those New England towns designed with such charm and quaintness that you would think that one mastermind had created it. It's one of those places that has to be on your tour of New England and the Jackson House, just outside town, is a great place for a stopover here. With its yellow exterior it just beckons you inside where you'll find great examples of late-Victorian architecture with floors of cherry and maple setting off the fine furniture, walls, and moldings. Its traditionally decorated guestrooms include six one-room luxury suites with fireplaces, thermal massage tubs, and views of the gardens. Period antiques are used throughout most of the inn, adding to your enjoyment. I loved the third-floor Francesca room, decorated in muted tones of taupe, with its deck overlooking the landscaped grounds. The Mary Todd Lincoln room is much more Victorian in feel, with a high-back Victorian bed of the Lincoln period, a marble-topped table, tufted-velvet chair, and an exquisite Casablanca ceiling fan of bronze, copper, rosewood, and French-cut crystal. The inn has a very fine dining room, which has garnered much praise. While I was visiting there was an announcement of a forthcoming wine-maker dinner—a great menu with accompanying wines. *Directions:* From Boston take I-93 to I-89, leaving at Route 4 west. Leave at exit 1 in Vermont for Woodstock. The inn is on the far side of the town on the right.

JACKSON HOUSE
Innkeepers: Gloria & Juan Florin
114–3 Senior Lane
Woodstock, VT 05091
Tel: (802) 457-2065 or (800) 448-1890
Fax: (802) 457-9290
E-mail: innkeepers@jacksonhouse.com
9 rooms, 6 suites, Double: $195–$340
Open all year
Credit cards: all major
Restaurant: breakfast & dinner
Handicap room

Index

1

1661 Inn & Hotel Manisses, The, Block Island, 156
1811 House, Manchester, 178

A

Abbot Village, 65
Acadia National Park, 57, 65
  Cadillac Mountain, 58
  Loop Road, 57
  Otter Cliffs, 58
  Schoodic Peninsula, 58
  Thunder Hole, 58
Adair, Bethlehem, 146
American Revolution, 33
Andover
  Rowell's Inn, 162
Antique Shops, Lower Maine, 51
Antiquing, 11
Arlington, 43
  West Mountain Inn, 163
Ashley Falls, 41
Ashley Manor, Barnstable, 112
Avon, 73

B

Bagley House Inn, The, Durham, 94
Bangor, 65
Bar Harbor, 58, 65
  Inn at Canoe Point, The, 86
  Manor House Inn, 87
  Ullikana, 88
Barnard
  Twin Farms, 164

Barnstable, 26
  Ashley Manor, 112
  Cobb's Cove Inn, 113
Barrows House, Dorset, 171
Bartlett, 67
Bath, 54
  Kennebec River Ride, 55
  Maine Maritime Museum, 54
Bathrooms, 2
Bee and Thistle Inn, Old Lyme, 81
Bennington, 42, 69
Bernardston, 70
Bethlehem, 67, 68
  Adair, 146
Blantyre, Lenox, 127
Block Island
  1661 Inn & Hotel Manisses, The, 156
Blue Hill, 65
  Blue Hill Inn, The, 89
Blue Hill Peninsula, 57, 65
Blueberry Hill, Goshen, 173
Boothbay Harbor, 55
Boston, 16, 70, 71
  Back Bay, 19
  Beacon Hill, 17
  Boston Common, 19
  Boston Garden, 19
  Boston Pops, 20
  Capitol Building, 17
  Charles Street Inn, The, 114, 22
  Charlestown
    USS Constitution, 21
  Children's Museum, 20
  Commonwealth Avenue, 19
  Copley Square, 19
  Faneuil Hall, 17

Boston, 16, 70, 71 (continued)
    Financial District, 19
    Freedom Trail, 17
    Harrison Gray Otis House, 18
    Isabella Stewart Gardner Museum, 19
    John Hancock Tower, 19
    Lenox, The, 115, 22
    Museum of Fine Arts, 19
    Museum of Science, 20
    New England Aquarium, 21
    Newbury Street, 17
    North End, 19
    Old South Meeting House, 17
    Old State House, 17
    Paul Revere House, 19
    Museum at the John F. Kennedy Library, 19
    Quincy Market, 17
    SPNEA Headquarters, 18
    State House, 18
    Subway, 17
        North Station, 17
        Park Street Station, 17
    Symphony Orchestra, 20
    Theatre District, 21
    Tourist Information, 21
    Trinity Church, 19
Boulders Inn, New Preston, 79
Brandon
    Lilac Inn, The, 165
Brattleboro, 69
Breakfast, 3
Bretton Woods, 67
Brewster, 26
    Captain Freeman Inn, The, 116
Bridgewater Corners
    October Country Inn, 166
Brunswick, 54, 65
    Bowdoin College, 54
        Museum of Art, 54

Bucksport, 65
Bufflehead Cove, Kennebunkport, 97
Burlington, 45, 68
Buttonwood Inn, The, North Conway, 153

C

Cambridge, 21
    Botanical Museum, 21
    Cambridge House, A, 117
    Harvard Memorial Church, 21
    Harvard Museums of Cultural and Natural History, 21
    Harvard University, 21
    Harvard Yard, 21
    Massachusetts Institute of Technology, 21
    Radcliffe College, 21
Camden, 56, 65
    Camden Windward House, 90
    Inn at Sunrise Point, The, 91
    Library, 56
    Main Street, 56
    Maine Stay, 92
Canaan, 73
Cancellation Policies, 3
Cape Ann, 51
Cape Cod, 26
Cape Cod Canal, 26
Cape Cod National Seashore, 27
Cape Porpoise, 52
Captain Farris House, South Yarmouth, 136
Captain Freeman Inn, The, Brewster, 116
Captain Lord Mansion, Kennebunkport, 98
Captain's House Inn, The, Chatham, 118
Car Rental, 12
Casco Bay, 53
Castle Hill Inn & Resort, Newport, 157
Charles Street Inn, The, Boston, 114, 22
Charlotte Inn, The, Edgartown, 123
Chatham, 27
    Captain's House Inn, The, 118

Check-in, 4
Chelsea
    Shire Inn, 167
Chester, 36, 44, 74
Chesterfield
    Chesterfield Inn, 147
Children, 4
Chittenden, 45
    Mountain Top Inn & Resort, 168
    Tulip Tree Inn, 169
Cliffside Inn, Newport, 158
Cobb's Cove Inn, Barnstable Village, 113
Cohasset, 25
Colchester, 74
Comfort, 4
Concord, 33, 70
    Concord's Colonial Inn, 119
    Hawthorne Inn, 120
    Museum, 34
    Old North Bridge, 33
    Old North Bridge Visitor Center, 33
    Orchard House, 34
    Ralph Waldo Emerson Home, 34
    Sleepy Hollow Cemetery, 34
    Walden Pond, 34
Connecticut River Valley, 35
Conway, 67
Copper Beech Inn,Ivoryton, 77
Cornucopia of Dorset, Dorset, 172
Cornwall Bridge, 73
Craftsbury Common
    Inn on the Common, The, 170
Crawford North, 67
Credit Cards, 5
Criteria for Selection, 5
Crocker House Country Inn, Hancock Point, 96

D

Damariscotta, 56

Danbury, 73
Daniel Webster Inn, Sandwich, 133
Deep River, 36, 74
Deer Isle, 57, 65
    Pilgrim's Inn, 93
Deerfield, 70
    Deerfield Inn, 121
Deerhill Inn, West Dover, 185
Dennis, 26
Desert of Maine, 54
Dockside Guest Quarters, York, 109
Dorset, 43, 68, 69
    Barrows House, 171
    Cornucopia of Dorset, 172
Dover, 65
Driving Times, 13
Durham
    Bagley House Inn, The, 94
Duxbury, 25

E

East Haddam, 36
    Goodspeed Opera House, 36
Eastham, 27
    Whalewalk Inn, The, 122
Edgartown
    Charlotte Inn, The, 123
    Hob Knob Inn, 124
    Point Way Inn, 125
Ellsworth, 65
Essex, 36, 51, 74
    Griswold Inn, 76

F

Falmouth
    Maison Cappellari at Mostly Hall, La, 126
Four Columns Inn, Newfane, 180
Francestown
    Inn at Crotched Mountain, The, 148

Franconia, 68
Freeport, 54
    L. L. Bean Store, 54

G

Glastonbury, 74
Glen, 67
Gloucester, 50
    Beauport, 50
    Cape Ann Historical Museum, 50
    Hammond Castle Museum, 50
Goose Cove Lodge, The, Sunset, 106
Goose Rocks, 52
Gorham, 67
Goshen, 45
    Blueberry Hill, 173
Grafton, 44
    Old Tavern, The, 174
Great Barrington, 41, 71
Green Guide to Antiquing in New England, 11
Green Mountain National Forest, 68, 69
Green Mountains, 44, 59
Greenfield, 70
Greenville, 59, 65
    Lodge at Moosehead Lake, The, 95
Grey Rock Inn, Northeast Harbor, 103
Griswold Inn, Essex, 76
Groton, 70

H

Hancock, 70
    Hancock Inn, The, 149
Hancock Point, Crocker House Country Inn, 96
Hancock Shaker Village, 42
Harbor Light Inn, The, Marblehead, 128
Hart's Location, 67
    Notchland Inn, The, 150
Hartford, 73, 74
Hartwell House, Ogunquit, 104

Hawthorne Inn, Concord, 120
Historic Jacob Hill Farm Bed and Breakfast Inn,
Providence, 159
Hob Knob Inn, Edgartown, 124
Holderness
    Manor on Golden Pond, The, 151
Hyannis, 27
    John F. Kennedy Summer Home, 27

I

Inn at Canoe Point, The, Bar Harbor, 86
Inn at Crotched Mountain, The, Francestown, 148
Inn at National Hall, The, Westport, 84
Inn at Ormsby Hill, The, Manchester Center, 177
Inn at Sawmill Farm, The, West Dover, 186
Inn at Shelburne Farms, The, Shelburne, 182
Inn at Stockbridge, The, Stockbridge, 137
Inn at Sunrise Point, The, Camden, 91
Inn at the Round Barn Farm, The, Waitsfield, 183
Inn at Thorn Hill, The, Jackson Village, 152
Inn at Weathersfield, The, Perkinsville, 181
Inn at Weston, The, Weston, 188
Inn on the Common, The, Craftsbury Common, 170
Innkeepers' Professionalism, 5
Introduction, 1
    About Inn Travel, 2
    About Itineraries, 10
Isaiah Jones Homestead, Sandwich, 134
Itineraries
    Boston: A Grand Beginning, 16
    Cape Cod, Nantucket, Martha's Vineyard & Newport, 24
    Route 7 & Much More, 38
    Sturbridge & the Connecticut Shore, 32
    The Byways of Coastal Maine, 48
    Fall Foliage Routes, 62
        Boston to Central Massachusetts, 70
        Boston to Western Massachusetts, 71
        Central & Western Connecticut, 73
        Coastal & Central Maine, 65

Fall Foliage Routes, 62 (continued)
    Daytrip from Hartford, 74
    Northern New Hampshire & Northern Vermont, 67
    Southern Vermont, 69
Ivoryton
    Copper Beech Inn, 77

J

Jackson House, Woodstock, 189
Jackson Village, 67
    Inn at Thorn Hill, The, 152
Jacob's Pillow Dance Festival, 42
Jaffrey, 70
Jamaica, 44
    Three Mountain Inn, 175

K

Kancamagus Highway, 68
Keene, 70
Kennebunkport, 52
    Bufflehead Cove, 97
    Captain Lord Mansion, 98
    George Bush Summer Home, 52
    Maine Stay Inn & Cottages, The, 99
    Old Fort Inn, 100
    White Barn Inn, 101
Kent, 73

L

Lancaster, 67
Ledyard
    Stonecroft Country Inn, 78
Lee, 71
Lenox, 71
    Blantyre, 127
Lenox, The, Boston, 115, 22
Lexington, 33, 70
Lilac Inn, The, Brandon, 165

Litchfield, 40
    First Congregational Church, 40
Littleton, 67
Lodge at Moosehead Lake, The, Greenville, 95
Londonderry, 69
Longfellow's Wayside Inn, Sudbury, 140
Lower Waterford, 68
    Rabbit Hill Inn, 176
Ludlow, 44
Lyme, 36

M

Maine Stay Inn & Cottages, The, Kennebunkport, 99
Maine Stay, Camden, 92
Maison Cappellari at Mostly Hall, La, Falmouth, 126
Manchester, 43, 68, 69
    1811 House, 178
Manchester Center, 43, 68, 69
    Inn at Ormsby Hill, The, 177
Manor House Inn, Bar Harbor, 87
Manor House, Norfolk, 80
Manor on Golden Pond, The, Holderness, 151
Maps–Itineraries, 13
    Overview Map of Itineraries, 15
    Cape Cod, Nantucket, Martha's Vineyard & Newport, 23
    Route 7 & Much More, 37
    Sturbridge & the Connecticut Shore, 31
    The Byways of Coastal Maine, 47
    Fall Foliage Routes
        Overview Map of Routes, 61
        Boston to Central Massachusetts, 70
        Boston to Western Massachusetts, 71
        Central & Western Connecticut, 72
        Coastal & Central Maine, 64
        Daytrip from Hartford, 74
        Northern New Hampshire & Northern Vermont, 66
        Southern Vermont, 69

Maps–Places to Stay
  Map 1, Connecticut, 75
  Map 2, Maine, 85
  Map 3, Massachusetts, 111
  Map 4, New Hampshire, 145
  Map 5, Rhode Island, 155
  Map 6, Vermont, 161
Marblehead, 50
  Harbor Light Inn, The, 128
Marlborough, 74
Martha's Place, Vineyard Haven, 141
Martha's Vineyard, 29
  Edgartown, 29
  Gay Head, 29
  Oak Bluffs, 29
  Vineyard Haven, 29
Mayflower II, 25
Mendon, 45
  Red Clover Inn, 179
Minuteman National Historic Park, 33
Minutemen, 33
Mohegan Island, 56
Montpelier, 68
Moosehead Lake, 65
Morgan's Way, Orleans, 131
Mount Desert Island, 57
Mount Equinox, 43
Mountain Top Inn & Resort, Chittenden, 168
Mystic Village Seaport, 35
  Charles W. Morgan, 35
  Children's Museum, 35
  Stillman Building, 35

N

Nantucket, 28
  Nantucket Historical Association, 28
  Old Gaol, 28
  Old Mill, 28
  Oldest House, 28

Nantucket, 28 (continued)
  Pineapple Inn, The, 129
  Seven Sea Street, 130
  Three Bricks, 28
  Whaling Museum, 28
New Canaan, 40
  Silvermine Guild of Artists, 40
New Hartford, 73
New Haven, 73
New Milford, 73
New Preston
  Boulders Inn, 79
Newburyport, 51
Newcastle, 56
  Newcastle Inn, The, 102
Newfane, 44, 69
  Four Columns Inn, 180
Newport, 29
  Castle Hill Inn & Resort, 157
  Cliffside Inn, 158
Norfolk, 73
  Manor House, 80
North Conway, 67
  Buttonwood Inn, The, 153
North Woodstock, 68
Northeast Harbor, 59, 65
  Grey Rock Inn, 103
Northfield, 70
Norwalk, 40
Notchland Inn, The, Hart's Location, 150

O

October Country Inn, Bridgewater Corners, 166
Ogunquit, 51
  Hartwell House, 104
Old Bennington, 42
  Battle Monument, 42
  Grandma Moses Schoolhouse, 42
  Old First Church, 42

Old Fort Inn, Kennebunkport, 100
Old Lyme, 36, 74
    Bee and Thistle Inn, 81
Old Saybrook, 74
Old Tavern, The, Grafton, 174
Orleans, 27
    Morgan's Way, 131

P

Pacing, 13
Palmer, 71
Paul Revere, 33
Penobscot Bay, 56
Perkinsville
    Inn at Weathersfield, The, 181
Peterborough, 70
Pilgrim's Inn, Deer Isle, 93
Pineapple Inn, The, Nantucket, 129
Pitcher Inn, The, Warren, 184
Pittsfield, 42
Plymouth, 25
    Mayflower II, 25
    Mayflower Society Museum, 25
    Pilgrim Hall Museum, 25
    Plymouth Rock, 25
Point Way Inn, Edgartown, 125
Pomegranate Inn, Portland, 105
Portland, 53
    Museum of Art, 53
    Pomegranate Inn, 105
Providence, 30
    Brown University, 30
    Historic Jacob Hill Farm Bed and Breakfast Inn, 159
    John Brown House, 30
    Rhode Island School of Design, 30
Provincetown, 27
Publick House Historic Inn, Sturbridge, 139

Q

Quincy, 25

R

Rabbit Hill Inn, Lower Waterford, 176
Red Clover Inn, Mendon, 179
Red Lion Inn, The, Stockbridge, 138
Reservations, 6
Responsibility, 6
Restaurants, 7
Ridgefield, 40, 73
    Aldrich Museum of Contemporary Art, 40
    West Lane Inn, 82
Rochester, 67
Rockland, 56
    Farnsworth Art Museum, 56
Rockport, 51
    Yankee Clipper Inn, 132
Room Rates, 7
Rowell's Inn, Andover, 162

S

Sagamore Bridge, 26
Salem, 49
    Chestnut Street, 50
    House of Seven Gables, 50
    Peabody Essex Museum, 49
    Pioneer Village, 50
    Witch Museum, 50
Salisbury, 40
    Under Mountain Inn, 83
Sandwich, 26
    Daniel Webster Inn, 133
    Glass Museum, 26
    Heritage Plantation Museum, 26
    Isaiah Jones Homestead, 134
Seven Sea Street, Nantucket, 130

Sheffield, 41
Shelburne, 45, 68
    Inn at Shelburne Farms, The, 182
    Museum, 45
Sherburne, 68
Shire Inn, Chelsea, 167
Smoking, 8
Socializing, 8
Society for the Preservation of New England Antiquities, 18, 50
South Canaan, 73
South Egremont
    Weathervane Inn, The, 135
South Mountain Concert Festival, 42
South Stoddard, 70
South Yarmouth
    Captain Farris House, 136
Southwest Harbor, 59, 65
Springfield, 71
Squire Tarbox Inn, The, Wiscasset, 108
St. Johnsbury, 68
Stockbridge, 41, 68, 71
    Berkshire Playhouse, 42
    Chesterwood, 42
    Inn at Stockbridge, The, 137
    Norman Rockwell Museum, 42
    Red Lion Inn, The, 138
Stonecroft Country Inn, Ledyard, 78
Stonington, 57, 65
Sturbridge, 35, 71
    Old Sturbridge Village, 35, 71
    Publick House Historic Inn, 139
Sudbury
    Longfellow's Wayside Inn, 140
Sunset, 57
    Goose Cove Lodge, The, 106
Surry, 65

T

Tanglewood Music Festival, 42
Thorncroft Inn, Vineyard Haven, 142
Three Mountain Inn, Jamaica, 175
Townshend, 44, 69, 70
Tulip Tree Inn, Chittenden, 169
Turners Falls, 70
Twin Farms, Barnard, 164
Twin Mountain, 67

U

Ullikana, Bar Harbor, 88
Under Mountain Inn, Salisbury, 83
USS Constitution, 21

V

Villa, The, Westerly, 160
Vineyard Haven
    Martha's Place, 141
    Thorncroft Inn, 142

W

Waitsfield, 45, 68
    Inn at the Round Barn Farm, The, 183
Warren, 45, 68
    Pitcher Inn, The, 184
Waterbury, 68
Waterford
    Waterford Inne, The, 107
Wauwinet
    Wauwinet, The, 143
Weather, 14
Weathervane Inn, The, South Egremont, 135
Website
    Karen Brown Website, 9
Wedding Cake House, nr Kennebunkport, 52
Wedgewood Inn, Yarmouth Port, 144
Wells, 52

West Cornwall, 73
West Dover
    Deerhill Inn, 185
    Inn at Sawmill Farm, The, 186
West Lane Inn, Ridgefield, 82
West Mountain Inn, Arlington, 163
West Rindge, 70
West Townshend, 44, 69
    Windham Hill Inn, 187
Westerly
    Villa, The, 160
Weston
    Inn at Weston, The, 188
Westport
    Inn at National Hall,The, 84
Whalewalk Inn, The, Eastham, 122
Wheelchair Accessibility, 9
White Barn Inn, Kennebunkport, 101
White Mountains, 59, 68
Williamstown, 42, 71
    Sterling and Francine Clark Institute, 42, 71
    Theatre, 42
Wilton, 73
Winchester, 70
Windham Hill Inn, West Townshend, 187
Wiscasset, 55, 65
    Squire Tarbox Inn, The, 108
Woodstock, 45
    Jackson House, 189

Y

Yankee Clipper Inn, Rockport, 132
Yarmouth Port, 26
    Wedgewood Inn, 144
York, 51
    Dockside Guest Quarters, 109
York Harbor, 51

Enhance Your Guides

Travel Your Dreams
Online

www.karenbrown.com

- Hotel News
- Color Photos
- New Discoveries
- Corrections & Edits
- Leisure Destinations
- Property of the Month
- Postcards from the Road
- Romantic Inns & Recipes

Become a Karen Brown Preferred Reader

Name _____

Street _____

Town _____

State _____ Zip _____ Country _____

Tel _____ Fax _____

E-mail _____

We'd love to welcome you as a Karen Brown Preferred Reader. Send us your name and address and you will be entered in our monthly drawing to receive a free set of Karen Brown guides. As a preferred reader, you will receive special promotions and be the first to know when new editions of Karen Brown guides go to press.

Please send to: Karen Brown's Guides, Post Office Box 70, San Mateo, California 94401, USA
tel: (650) 342-9117, fax: (650) 342-9153, e-mail: karen@karenbrown.com, website: www: karenbrown.com

SHARE YOUR DISCOVERIES WITH US

Outstanding properties often come from readers' discoveries. We would love to hear from you.

Please list below any hotel or bed & breakfast you discover. Tell us what you liked about the property and, if possible, please include a brochure or photographs so we can share your enthusiasm. We keep a permanent database of all of your recommendations for future use. Note: we regret we cannot return photos.

Owner _____ Hotel or B&B _____

Address _____ Town _____ Country _____

Comments:

Your name _____ Street _____

Town _____ State _____ Zip _____ Country _____

Tel _____ E-mail _____ Date _____

Do we have your permission to electronically publish your comments on our website? Yes _____ No _____

If yes, would you like to remain anonymous? Yes ___No ___ , or may we use your name? Yes___ No___

Please send report to: Karen Brown's Guides, Post Office Box 70, San Mateo, California 94401, USA
tel: (650) 342-9117, fax: (650) 342-9153, e-mail: karen@karenbrown.com, www.karenbrown.com

CRITIQUE PLACES IN OUR BOOK

We greatly appreciate first-hand evaluations of places in our guides so your critiques are invaluable to us. To stay current on the properties in our guides, we keep a database of readers' comments. To keep our readers up to date, we also sometimes share feedback with them via our website.

Please list your comments on properties that you have visited. We welcome accolades, as well as criticisms.

Name of Hotel or B&B _____

Town _____ Country _____

Comments:

Your name _____ Street _____

Town _____ State _____ Zip _____ Country _____

Tel _____ E-mail _____ Date _____

Do we have your permission to electronically publish your comments on our website? Yes _____ No _____

If yes, would you like to remain anonymous? Yes ___No ___, or may we use your name? Yes___ No___

Please send report to: Karen Brown's Guides, Post Office Box 70, San Mateo, California 94401, USA
tel: (650) 342-9117, fax: (650) 342-9153, e-mail: karen@karenbrown.com, www.karenbrown.com

KB Travel Service

❖ **KB Travel Service** offers travel planning assistance using itineraries designed by *Karen Brown* and published in her guidebooks. We will customize any itinerary to fit your personal interests.

❖ We will plan your itinerary with you, help you decide how long to stay and what to do once you arrive, and work out the details.

❖ We will book your airline tickets and your rental car, arrange rail tickets or passes (including your seat reservations), reserve accommodations recommended in *Karen Brown's Guides,* and supply you with point-to-point information and consultation.

Contact us to start planning your travel!

800 782-2128 ext. 328 or e-mail: info@kbtravelservice.com

Service fees do apply

KB Travel Service
16 East Third Avenue
San Mateo, CA 94401 USA
www.kbtravelservice.com

Independently owned and operated by Town & Country Travel
CST 2001543-10

is the
Preferred Airline
of
Karen Brown's Guides

auto ⊕ europe.

Karen Brown's

Preferred Car Rental Service Provider

When Traveling to Europe
for

International Car Rental Services
Chauffeur & Transfer Services
Prestige & Sports Cars
Motor Home Rentals

1-800-223-5555

Be sure to identify yourself as a Karen Brown Traveler.
For special offers and discounts use your
Karen Brown ID number 99006187.

Seal Cove Inn

Located in the San Francisco Bay Area

Karen Brown Herbert (best known as author of the Karen Brown's guides) and her husband, Rick, have put 22 years of experience into reality and opened their own superb hideaway, Seal Cove Inn. Spectacularly set amongst wild flowers and bordered by towering cypress trees, Seal Cove Inn looks out to the distant ocean over acres of county park: an oasis where you can enjoy secluded beaches, explore tidepools, watch frolicking seals, and follow the tree-lined path that traces the windswept ocean bluffs. Country antiques, original watercolors, flower-laden cradles, rich fabrics, and the gentle ticking of grandfather clocks create the perfect ambiance for a foggy day in front of the crackling log fire. Each bedroom is its own haven with a cozy sitting area before a wood-burning fireplace and doors opening onto a private balcony or patio with views to the park and ocean. Moss Beach is a 35-minute drive south of San Francisco, 6 miles north of the picturesque town of Half Moon Bay, and a few minutes from Princeton harbor with its colorful fishing boats and restaurants. Seal Cove Inn makes a perfect base for whale-watching, salmon-fishing excursions, day trips to San Francisco, exploring the coast, or, best of all, just a romantic interlude by the sea, time to relax and be pampered. Karen and Rick look forward to the pleasure of welcoming you to their coastal hideaway.

Seal Cove Inn • 221 Cypress Avenue • Moss Beach • California • 94038 • USA
tel: (650) 728-4114, fax: (650) 728-4116, e-mail: sealcove@coastside.net, website: sealcoveinn.com

Travel Your Dreams • Order your Karen Brown Guides Today

Please ask in your local bookstore for Karen Brown's Guides. If the books you want are unavailable, you may order directly from the publisher. Books will be shipped immediately.

_____ *Austria: Charming Inns & Itineraries* $19.95

_____ *California: Charming Inns & Itineraries* $19.95

_____ *England: Charming Bed & Breakfasts* $18.95

_____ *England, Wales & Scotland: Charming Hotels & Itineraries* $19.95

_____ *France: Charming Bed & Breakfasts* $18.95

_____ *France: Charming Inns & Itineraries* $19.95

_____ *Germany: Charming Inns & Itineraries* $19.95

_____ *Ireland: Charming Inns & Itineraries* $19.95

_____ *Italy: Charming Bed & Breakfasts* $18.95

_____ *Italy: Charming Inns & Itineraries* $19.95

_____ *New England: Charming Inns & Itineraries* $19.95

_____ *Portugal: Charming Inns & Itineraries* $19.95

_____ *Spain: Charming Inns & Itineraries* $19.95

_____ *Switzerland: Charming Inns & Itineraries* $19.95

Name _____ Street _____

Town _____ State _____ Zip _____ Tel _____

Credit Card (MasterCard or Visa) _____ Expires: _____

For orders in the USA, add $4 for the first book and $1 for each additional book for shipment. California residents add 8.25% sales tax. Overseas orders add $10 per book for airmail shipment. Indicate number of copies of each title; fax or mail form with check or credit card information to:

KAREN BROWN'S GUIDES
Post Office Box 70 • San Mateo • California • 94401 • USA
tel: (650) 342-9117, fax: (650) 342-9153, e-mail: karen@karenbrown.com
You can also order directly from our website at www.karenbrown.com.

KAREN BROWN wrote her first travel guide in 1977. Her personalized travel series has grown to fourteen titles which Karen and her small staff work diligently to keep updated. Karen, her husband, Rick, and their children, Alexandra and Richard, live in Moss Beach, a small town on the coast south of San Francisco. They settled here in 1991 when they opened Seal Cove Inn. Karen is frequently traveling, but when she is home, in her role as innkeeper, enjoys welcoming Karen Brown readers.

JACK BULLARD grew up in New England and after completing his graduate education there spent fifteen years in international consulting in marketing and finance, and then ten years as executive director of two Boston law firms. Moving to southern California in 1988, he managed another law firm before purchasing The Inn at Occidental in the Sonoma wine country in 1994 and transforming it into one of California's most highly rated inns north of San Francisco.

VANESSA KALE, who produced all of the inn sketches and delightful illustrations in this guide, knew from early childhood that she wanted to be an artist. A native of Bellingham, Washington, Vanessa spent her high school years in Sonoma, California. After graduating in Art from UC Davis, Vanessa moved to Sherman Oaks, California where she works as a freelance artist.

JANN POLLARD, the artist responsible for the beautiful painting on the cover of this guide, has studied art since childhood, and is well known for her outstanding impressionistic-style watercolors, which she has exhibited in numerous juried shows, winning many awards. Jann travels frequently to Europe (using Karen Brown's guides) where she loves to paint historic buildings. Jann lives in Burlingame, California, with her husband, Gene.

Notes